SURREY
RAILWAYS
Remembered

Leslie Oppitz

COUNTRYSIDE BOOKS
NEWBURY, BERKSHIRE

Also by Leslie Oppitz:
Sussex Railways Remembered

TO JEAN
Whose idea started it all

First Published 1988
© Leslie Oppitz 1988

COUNTRYSIDE BOOKS
3 CATHERINE ROAD
NEWBURY, BERKSHIRE

ISBN 1 85306 005 4

Produced through MRM (Print Consultants) Ltd., Reading
Typeset by Acorn Bookwork, Salisbury, Wilts
Printed in England

Contents

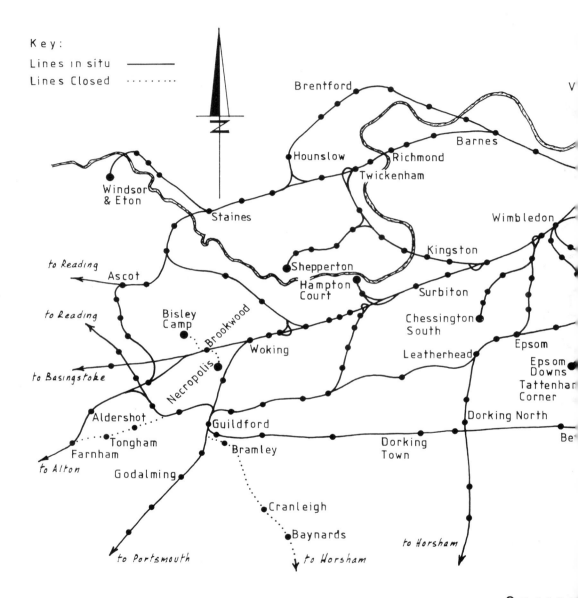

Key:
Lines in situ ———
Lines Closed ·········

Brentford
Barnes
Hounslow
Richmond
Twickenham
Windsor & Eton
Staines
Wimbledon
Kingston
to Reading
Ascot
Shepperton
Hampton Court
Surbiton
Bisley Camp
Brookwood
Chessington South
Epsom
to Reading
Woking
Leatherhead
Epsom Downs
to Basingstoke
Necropolis
Tattenham Corner
Aldershot
Guildford
Dorking North
Tongham
Bramley
Dorking Town
Be
Farnham
to Alton
Godalming
to Portsmouth
Cranleigh
Baynards
to Horsham
to Horsham

S u r r e y

4

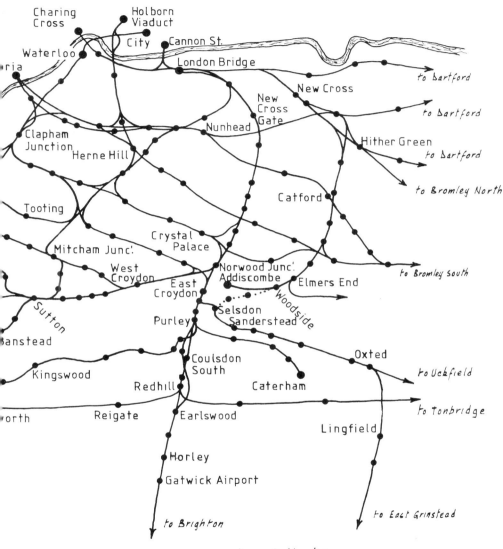

Charing
Cross

Holborn
Viaduct

City

Cannon St.

Waterloo

London Bridge

to Dartford

...ria

New Cross

to Dartford

New
Cross
Gate

Nunhead

Hither Green

to Dartford

Clapham
Junction

Herne Hill

to Bromley North

Tooting

Catford

Crystal
Palace

Mitcham Junc:

West
Croydon

Norwood Junc:
Addiscombe

to Bromley South

East
Croydon

Elmers End

Sutton

Purley

Woodside

Selsdon
Sanderstead

...anstead

Oxted

Coulsdon
South

Kingswood

to Uckfield

Redhill

Caterham

...orth

Reigate

Earlswood

to Tonbridge

Lingfield

Horley

Gatwick Airport

to East Grinstead

to Brighton

Brian Butler '87

R a i l w a y s

5

ACKNOWLEDGEMENTS

Thanks are due to the many members of BR staff who have given valuable assistance during my travels around Surrey and to British Rail (Southern) Press Office at Waterloo for their helpful information. In particular, thanks go to J.L. Smith at 'Lens of Sutton' whose patience enabled me to acquire numerous early pictures. Acknowledgements go also to many libraries throughout Surrey, particularly the Local Studies Sections at Guildford and Croydon who never failed to produce an answer.

A special mention goes to the *Croydon Advertiser* Group of Newspapers for their encouragement in publishing many of my early railway articles.

Not to be forgotten are the numerous Oakwood Press publications where in-depth studies have given invaluable guidance where previously very little material has been available.

Personal thanks are due to Norman Edwards, a member of the 'Brighton Circle', who assisted with his excellent knowledge of steam locomotives.

Finally thanks go to Joan, my wife, who gave considerable assistance and encouragement and also proved herself very capable as a proof reader!

Leslie Oppitz

The following abbreviations are used on numerous occasions in this book:

Abbreviation	Full title
CM&G	Croydon, Merstham & Godstone Iron Railway
CO&EGR	Croydon, Oxted & East Grinstead Railway
GER	Great Eastern Railway
GWR	Great Western Railway
L&BR	London & Brighton Railway
L&CR	London & Croydon Railway
L&GR	London & Greenwich Railway
LBSCR	London, Brighton and South Coast Railway (often referred to as 'the Brighton company')
LCDR	London, Chatham & Dover Railway
LNC	London Necropolis Company
LNER	London & North Eastern Railway
LNWR	London & North Western Railway
LSWR	London & South Western Railway
M&TVR	Metropolitan & Thames Valley Railway
S&SJR	Surrey & Sussex Junction Railway
SECR	South Eastern & Chatham Railway (the working union of the SER & LCDR from 1899)
SER	South Eastern Railway
SIR	Surrey Iron Railway

INTRODUCTION

At the start of the last century no railways existed in Southern England. Passenger travel and movement of freight was by road, canal or by coastal vessels. In Surrey one of the first turnpikes was a trust established in 1696 covering a road from Reigate to Crawley in Sussex. More were to follow and by 1770 a turnpike was established from London to Brighton. Canals had been dug in the early 1800s adding to the rivers already made navigable but transport was slow and none of these ventures was financially successful.

In the opening years of the 19th century, Britain was at war with Napoleon and it was the need to divert vessels from the perilous Dover Straits that brought about a scheme to link the important naval base of Portsmouth with London. When France was defeated at Trafalgar in 1805 the danger to Channel shipping lessened but the need for such a commercial link remained.

It was in this climate that the world's first public railway came into existence. Intended to reach Portsmouth from the capital, there was a proposal to open a route, partly by rail and partly by canal. Initially the first section from the Thames at Wandsworth was to have been canal but it was decided that such a move would be harmful to the industries of the Wandle valley. Instead the 8 mile long Surrey Iron Railway from Wandsworth to Croydon was built. Within two years the Croydon, Merstham & Godstone Railway had linked Croydon with lime quarries at Merstham.

Activities now moved northwards following George Stephenson's enthusiasm over locomotive engines. With the opening of the Stockton to Darlington Railway in 1825, the first steam train had arrived. In the same year an Act was granted for the Canterbury & Whitstable Railway to be built. In 1826 a line between Liverpool and Manchester was approved and three years later the famous Rainhill trials took place to establish which type of steam locomotive gave the best means of traction.

Travelling was pretty uncomfortable in those early days. Railway carriages began as stage-coach bodies attached to waggon bases. They were small, cramped and unlit and had no heating or travel facilities. When lighting came it was by oil lamps, subsequently to be replaced by gas lamps. Steam heating and comfortable seating came late in the century and the 1880s saw the introduction of dining cars with kitchens equipped purpose-built for long distance travel. It is a sad reflection that the luxuries of Pullman car travel are today almost defunct!

In 1836 the London & Croydon Railway purchased the failing Croydon Canal for £40,250. Construction of the railway pushed ahead quickly, much of it along the old canal bed. The line was completed in 1839. A route southwards to Brighton was already under consideration and it was a proposal submitted by Sir John Rennie that was finally adopted.

By the 1840s railway lines were spreading rapidly across the county. Because of competition, the canals had no hope and all were to be abandoned commercially by the end of the century.

Despite the improved roadway systems, it became quicker and easier to move freight by rail. Freight depots were built and goods trafffic became a feature at almost every station. Few stations, however small, were without a number of sidings as business continued to increase. Truly the railways had arrived!

In more recent times, Surrey remains unique in the south east of England since, during the extensive cuts of the 1950s and 1960s, very few lines were affected. In fact, most of the lines north of the old SER route from Tonbridge in Kent to Reading in Berkshire remain relatively untouched.

In writing *Surrey Railways Remembered* therefore, the emphasis is on the lines as they were, from their early origins to their usage since their opening. Several lines have of course disappeared such as the Necropolis branch and Bisley Camp branch both leaving the main line at Brookwood, near Woking. The Horsham to Guildford branch closed in 1965 and the short route through Ash Green and Tongham (near Aldershot) was closed to passengers in July 1937. The stretch from Woodside to Selsdon was abandoned as recently as May 1983.

From the early days of the Surrey Iron Railway at the beginning of the last century, the book takes the reader through the early struggles over routes south from London Bridge ('Through Croydon to the South') including the battles in 1839 between the London & Greenwich Railway and the London & Croydon Railway to gain access to London Bridge station. Subsequently it follows the experimental days of atmospheric trains ('Trains that ran on air!') and then on to early ideas of electric trains from the year 1901 when there were plans for a monorail system from London to Brighton.

The ensuing chapters include many major routes and branch lines of historical interest and these are placed in chronological order as far as opening dates to various sections of track allow. Highlighted are details of the many bitter battles between the different railway companies. In the east the LBSCR and the SER had many serious disputes over territories. At one stage these appeared resolved by an 1848 agreement, but the troubles went on for many years. To the west the LBSCR and the LSWR had frequent problems culminating at one stage in December 1858 when a Guildford train became involved in the famous 'Battle of Havant' (Chapter 5).

For the sake of historical background the earlier county borders of Surrey (before the 1965 changes) have been taken into consideration. Also, to include the earlier Gatwick days, the Local Government re-organisation of 1974 which placed Gatwick in West Sussex has been disregarded.

Chapter 1

AN IRON RAILWAY REACHES MERSTHAM

Throughout the centuries Croydon has been a thriving market town of some importance. For a lengthy period, the town was bounded by large areas of forest and it was here that the practice of charcoal-burning developed. At that time, charcoal, then commonly known as 'coal', provided fuel for domestic heating. With London needing such supplies for its own requirements – and the many banquets of the day – it was becoming increasingly necessary to introduce an improved transportation system. The roads were generally poor, usually rutted or potted, and frequently thick with mud in poor weather.

However, it was not until the beginning of the 19th century that a decision was taken by local industrialists to promote a railway from the Thames at Wandsworth to Croydon – and later beyond – although earlier a canal had been envisaged. The canal idea was dropped since it would have proved detrimental to the river-based industries which utilised mills and works dependent on the river to provide their power.

An Act agreeing to the construction of the Surrey Iron Railway (SIR) was agreed by Parliament on 21st May 1801 and the subsequent Croydon, Merstham & Godstone Railway on 17th May 1803. The SIR, to be used for the pulling of freight, was to be the first such public railway in the world.

The eight miles of track from Wandsworth to Croydon officially opened on July 26th 1803. Horses or large mules pulled

The line from West Croydon to Mitcham Junction bears right off the main Sutton line, its course following much of the old Surrey Iron Railway route. (Author)

9

four-wheeled waggons transported either singly or coupled into 'trains'. Their loads included coal, iron, copper, bricks, grain and oilseeds.

The track was mostly double, using plate rails mounted on stone blocks. There was 4 ft 2 ins between the upturned flanges which guided the waggons' wheels. The section was available to the public on payment of a toll which permitted merchants or carriers to use their own waggons or horses. There is no evidence of passenger services on the Iron Railway on a regular basis but it is quite possible that waggons were cleaned out and sometimes used for excursions or organised outings.

Little evidence remains today of this pioneer route. The terminus at Wandsworth was formerly a canal basin in the area of the river Wandle, Armoury Way and Fairfield Street. From here the track struck south to Summerstown, crossing where a railway line today exists at Earlsfield. From the west side of Lambeth Cemetery the track continued along Mead Path and near Grove Road to the present Colliers Wood station. Here the charcoal burners of the past are remembered since they were known as 'colliers'.

After passing along part of Church Road and crossing Baron Walk, the line met the (present-day) A217 at Mitcham station. From here the original railway crossed Mitcham Common following a south-easterly direction to West Croydon, much of it along the course of today's Wimbledon to Croydon railway. At Waddon Marsh station the course leaves the present railway line to follow Factory Lane, close to the gasworks.

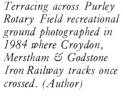

Terracing across Purley Rotary Field recreational ground photographed in 1984 where Croydon, Merstham & Godstone Iron Railway tracks once crossed. (Author)

The Croydon terminus was finally reached at an area known as Reeves Corner where Tamworth Road, Cairo New Road and Church Road meet – close to a new bridge. From this terminus a separate iron railway was built to link the SIR terminus with the basin of Croydon Canal not far away. Close to the present West

Croydon railway line, 132, Waddon New Road stands isolated, having been once considered to be a tollhouse for the SIR. To the north side a bricked-up window still exists where it was thought tolls from the passing waggons were collected. But later research suggests this property was built around 1852 for use with a coal depot and siding.

By June 1804, a short branch line was opened from Mitcham (Willow Lane Bridge) to Hackbridge. The track bore southwards for one and a quarter miles to follow the London Road (A237) past the Skinners Arms then curving to follow Hackbridge Road before crossing Hack Bridge. The original bridge of cast iron segments was demolished in 1912 and has since twice been replaced, the last time in 1983. The trains terminated close to the Wandle and opposite the site of Shepley Mills, just north of the present Carshalton to Hackbridge line.

The mills were probably once used for fulling wool but by the late 17th century they were manufacturing gunpowder. There were four mills although by 1744 three had become copper mills, rolling out copper sheet. The fourth was used for grinding dyewoods but this was converted to an oil mill which was later served by a siding from the Iron Railway where waggons brought in supplies of oilseeds.

The Hackbridge branch is said to have survived until 1846 by which time the conventional railways were taking over. Little evidence remains of the old line. The many stone sleeper blocks used in The Grove, Carshalton, probably came from the Shepley Mills area though the rails that have been displayed for many years outside Wallington library apparently came from stone mines at Godstone.

Much of the Croydon, Merstham & Godstone Iron Railway (CM&G) was single track although it was doubled for at least part of its existence. It opened officially in July 1805, with its terminus at the Croydon end forming an end-on junction with the Surrey Iron Railway from Wandsworth. The CM&G was originally intended to include a 'main line' to Reigate as the first stage of an extension to Portsmouth but the subsequent victory by Nelson at Trafalgar removed the French threat to Channel shipping and there was no further need. The line eventually only reached the stone mines at Quarry Dean, Merstham. Typical loads included chalk, lime, fuller's earth, timber and firestone.

No real trace of the CM&G remains through Croydon but the line existed along Tramway Road (now called Church Road). From close to the A23 at the Swan and Sugar Loaf, South Croydon, it passed across Haling Park to follow west of the Brighton Road through to Purley. Here the Rotary Field is well worth a visit. Not only has a short length of track been preserved in a railed-off area, but the centre path across the field is noticeably terraced, being part of the original permanent way.

Chipstead Valley was crossed by an overbridge. There is no evidence of this today but part of the embankment remains which can be located close to an Elim Chapel. After passing through the grounds of Cane Hill Hospital, the line crossed the A23 at the junction of Hollyme Oak Road and Wood Place Lane. Further south at Hooley, certain of the houses built on the east side of the A23 were constructed on surplus earth from the necessary railway cuttings.

Clear evidence of a brick parapet and abutments of an over-bridge can be seen from the A23 (just before the M23 turn-off) on the north side of Dean Lane immediately next to the 'Happy Eater'. Here enquiring historians can delight with refreshments very close to the original bridge where the track was sited. Unfortunately for posterity, the motorway has destroyed much of the remaining evidence but by staying on the old A23 a deep overgrown cutting which has existed for many years can be seen opposite Harps Oak Lane.

The line finally swung east from the road to pass behind the *Jolliffe Arms* – so named for its association with the Jolliffe family. W.J. Jolliffe, brother of the Squire of Merstham, went into partnership with Edward Banks in 1807 to set up the contracting firm of Jolliffe and Banks and it is believed to be this firm that built the nearby Weighbridge Cottage, used as a CM&G weigh-house and toll house. Just to the south of the *Jolliffe Arms* a short section of CM&G track stood for a long time in a railed-off area but this was stolen in 1982. However, rails exist today (taken from the Godstone mines) in a small garden across the road from *The Feathers* in Merstham. Neither of these locations of course represented the true track route.

In a booklet called *Retracing the First Public Railway*, Derek Bayliss writes of exciting finds in the Merstham area in the last twenty years or so. In 1961 a straight set of stone sleepers was discovered in situ in the lane between the *Jolliffe Arms* and the quarries and in 1967 in the Quarry Dean area over two yards of track was found at a depth of 2½ feet. It was considered that

Remains of an overbridge and abutments used on the Croydon, Merstham and Godstone Iron Railway next to the Happy Eater at Hooley. (Author)

more track lay below the farm road so in 1971/2 before the
motorway was built over the site, the Surrey Archaeological
Society excavated a length of 200 metres including parts of
sidings serving stone mines. One of these was on a gradient of
1 in 15, which must have been worked by winch.

With the Croydon Canal closing in 1836 and with eventual
competition from steam trains, it was inevitable that these early
railways should lose business. In 1837 the London & Brighton
Railway required two stretches of the CM&G south of Coulsdon
for its new line to the coast but by an Act dated July 15th 1837,
the L&BR was required to purchase the whole company. In
September 1838, the L&BR agreed to pay £9,614·8s to the
CM&G plus £1,000 to compensate for loss of profits. With
business almost at a standstill, the latter could indeed be considered generous! The CM&G was wound up in July 1839
although it may have been 1842 before the bulk of the track was
removed.

Traffic on the SIR from Wandsworth to Croydon came to an
end on August 31st 1846. The company's terminus at Croydon
was sold to the Croydon and Epsom Railway but the transaction
was delayed since it was found that the SIR had never paid for it
in the first place! This was later resolved with the sale going
through to the London, Brighton & South Coast Railway
(LBSCR) who had meantime taken over the Croydon and Epsom
company. The remaining land between Croydon and Mitcham,
owned by the SIR, was subsequently sold to adjacent landowners
and the Wandsworth dock area was sold by auction.

But this was not quite the end. In 1853 a branch line from
West Croydon to Wimbledon was authorised by Parliament and
by 1855 conventional trains were using the original SIR route
between Waddon Marsh and Mitcham. In order to do this, the
railway company had to buy back the sections of trackbed that
the SIR had sold.

Chapter 2

STEAM COMES TO CROYDON AND THE SOUTH

Parliament agreed to the construction of a canal linking the Thames at Rotherhithe with Croydon in 1801 in the same year that the Surrey Iron Railway had been approved. The canal took many years to build and final completion was not until October 1809. The total cost amounted to £127,000 and throughout its 9¼ miles length, some 28 locks were necessary.

The Croydon Canal, as it became known, had little success and shareholders had no return for their money. It had been necessary to build reservoirs at Sydenham and South Norwood and also a pumping station at Croydon to maintain water levels. Despite this, leakages often left the canal short of water.

In 1834 Joseph Gibbs carried out a survey for a new railway line from London to Croydon which could make use of sections of the canal bed. His report was accepted by the board of the proposed London & Croydon Railway who made an immediate offer for the canal's purchase. The offer was rejected and it was not until 1836, after settlement by a jury, that a figure of £40,250 was agreed. Navigation on the canal ceased in August of that year.

The London & Croydon Railway (L&CR) immediately went ahead with construction, building much of the track from Anerley to West Croydon (opened as 'Croydon') along the old canal bed. The station at West Croydon was built on the site of the canal basin and warehouses.

By the time the line opened on June 5th 1839, complications

Central Croydon Station at Katharine Street which opened in January 1868 to give passengers closer access to the town's shops. The idea was not successful and the station finally closed in August 1890. (Lens of Sutton)

had arisen. One of these was the need to share London Bridge station with another company, the London and Greenwich Railway (L&GR). In consequence it was necessary to pay the L&GR tolls per passenger when using their lines between Corbetts Junction (north of New Cross Gate Station) and London Bridge. This was unavoidable since the L&CR's terminus was the wrong side of the L&GR's station at London Bridge.

A late 1930s picture of East Croydon. SR No. 2039 hauls a goods set but on the right No. 7755 LMS (ex-LNER) Webb 0-6-2 'Coal Tank' built in 1884. (Lens of Sutton)

To this day London Bridge remains broken into different sections as dictated by the early railway planning. Eventually in 1840 the companies agreed to exchange buildings since the toll system was needlessly complicated to operate. To carry this out, the original Greenwich-owned station – it was apparently a crude affair – required considerable enlargement. This was completed in 1842 at the expense of the L&CR and also the SER and the L&BR who were now using the terminus. The stations were finally exchanged in 1844. At the southern end of the L&CR line, the Croydon company's offices were based at where West Croydon station is located today. These offices later became the station-master's office but today they no longer exist having been demolished when the Southern Railway came into being in 1923.

Some remaining difficulties at London Bridge were simplified when, in 1845, the South Eastern Railway (SER) took over the Greenwich Railway. This was coupled with proposals that the lines into the terminus should be widened to avoid further hostilities. But battles and complications continued.

The London & Brighton Railway received Parliamentary approval to build a line from Norwood to Brighton on July 15th 1837, the stretch from Norwood to Reigate (now Redhill) to be in agreement with the SER. The line took three years to complete. At times over 6,000 men and 960 horses were being used – many of the men being navvies from Ireland. Numerous routes had been suggested and it was finally one proposed by Sir John Rennie that was adopted.

The digging of the cuttings and embankments proved arduous. Barrows were filled and then hauled by horses one by one up plank walks to the top. The navvies had no living quarters and each had to make a rough shelter of turf and brushwood for protection. These were continually rebuilt as work progressed along the line. Fighting was prevalent especially on paydays when much drink was consumed. There were strike threats when no beer could be purchased near the site and boys were often paid ½d a journey to bring in supplies.

When Merstham tunnel was dug, it was found to be riddled with disused mining galleries. In March 1840, one of these was struck by workmen, releasing a flood of water which swept away wooden supports. Part of the works collapsed and a worker was killed. When the tunnel was completed, trains could reach as far as Haywards Heath. Beyond this station was Folly Hill Tunnel where construction problems still existed. From Haywards Heath to Brighton it was necessary to travel by special coach 'due to engineering works'. (Sounds familiar, doesn't it?) The line was finally completed on September 21st 1841.

The first train to run the whole journey left Brighton at 6.45 am to arrive at London Bridge one hour 45 minutes later. A special train carrying the Directors and their friends left at 8.45 am. There were 14 coaches pulled by two engines. To start with trains were first class only – to deter trippers – but there were usually two second class compartments in the front coach for servants.

East Croydon in the early 1950s. On the left BR No. 42089, Fairburn 2-6-4T next to an ex-GWR 3300 Bulldog class 4-4-0 – probably an enthusiasts' special. (Lens of Sutton)

A critic of the day wrote that 'the train got into a rapid motion and whizzed through the cuttings and over the embankments, both of considerable magnitude'. Others said that passengers who were hurtled through the air at speeds up to 30 mph would suffer epilepsy, hysteria and many other ailments. They said that railway staff could expect to spend time in hospital due to the strain of their dreadful working conditions.

When third class travel was introduced it was frequently in open trucks without seats. By 1845 an Act of Parliament compelled the railway companies to provide coaches which were covered. Before this happened a jeweller made his name by selling special railway spectacles as proof against the dirt and steam!

The Brighton Company were soon unhappy with dependence on the L&CR for access to London and considered the building of an independent line to Vauxhall in an involvement with yet another company, the London & South Western Railway (LSWR). Meantime the Croydon company and the SER joined forces to construct a new branch to a terminus at Bricklayer's Arms (named after a local hostelry) and invited the Brighton Company to participate. The station was called 'West End Terminus' because it was considered that access to the West End was easier from the new station than from London Bridge.

The venture proved disastrous. The Brighton company turned down the offer, still being interested in an involvement with the LSWR. The new station at Bricklayer's Arms opened on May 1st 1844, but it was not to last. The Croydon company withdrew its trains on March 31st 1845, and only half the SER trains now used the new terminus. The station finally closed to passengers in 1852 but remains a goods station to this day.

Bitter feelings remained between the Croydon and Brighton companies and it was reported that the latter gave instructions that if any Croydon Railway trains were waiting at the Jolly Sailor station (Norwood Junction) then they should be reversed into sidings to give any Brighton company train priority!

A major row had also broken out between the Brighton company and the SER over the required 'agreement' covering the line from Norwood to Redhill. Following an Act of Parliament of 1839, the SER obtained the power to purchase from the L&BR the stretch between Coulsdon and Redhill. When completed the cost was calculated at over £350,000 but the SER reckoned that it

LBSCR Marsh 13 4-4-2T No. 81 at South Croydon c1912. In the background, B2 4-4-0 'Smeaton' named after the famous engineer. (Lens of Sutton)

A Stroudley B1 (Gladstone) class locomotive No. 195 with passenger set arrives at Coulsdon and Cane Hill station c1910. (Lens of Sutton)

had been overcharged at more than £22,000 a mile! In addition it was critical of the Brighton company for building Merstham tunnel without a firm contract.

Bitter arguments ensued and it was not until July 1845, that an SER offer of £340,000 was accepted by the Brighton board. But this did not include the purchase of a gasworks already built to illuminate Merstham tunnel and the SER directors refused to take possession of it. The Brighton company was now not interested in lighting the tunnel so eventually the gasworks was sold to Lewes station where, at the time, exorbitant amounts were being paid to a local gas company to light the station.

Tunnel lighting had been a feature of the Brighton line both during its construction and when it was opened. Gas lamps had been fitted to the walls of Merstham tunnel which had also been whitewashed so that the new passengers could feel comforted in the dark. But the idea did not work for long because as the train passed through, the smoke blackened walls and the draught caused by the coaches blew out the lamps!

Meantime the arguments between the Croydon and Brighton companies continued. It was only when the Brighton company planned another route to London via Wandsworth that the Croydon company's hand was forced. Eventually the two agreed to amalgamation and in July 1846, the London, Brighton & South Coast Railway (LBSCR) was created.

In January 1868, Croydon acquired a fourth railway station. West Croydon had long since been established and East Croydon had opened when the Brighton line had commenced services to Haywards Heath in July 1841. South Croydon had opened in 1865. The new station, initially called 'Central Croydon', was built by the LBSCR with much encouragement from the local Council. It was constructed as a short spur from East Croydon (then called 'New Croydon') passing under Park Lane to reach Catherine Street (as it was then spelled). Plans were in hand to discontinue Croydon Fair after 1867 (held each year since 1276) and this meant that Fair Field had become available for railway use. The station opened on January 1st 1868. Double track was built with the terminus consisting of two side platforms plus numerous sidings. The platform buildings were constructed beyond the track area since there were no intentions of extending the line.

The object of the short branch was to give closer access to the shops but, with New Croydon not far away, it did not prove successful. Consequently the service was withdrawn on December 1st 1871, although the actual line and station remained and may well have been used as sidings. As commercial activity grew in Croydon there was another move by the Croydon Council to provide a passenger train service to the shops. In consequence the station was refurbished and a service restarted on June 1st 1886.

When re-opened, some records say its name had been changed to 'Croydon Central' but further research does not support this. Initially a number of London & North Western Railway (LNWR) trains used the station running via Crystal Palace to and from Willesden Junction and in the following year Great Eastern Railway (GER) trains used Central Croydon via the East London line to and from Liverpool Street. Despite these efforts and also possibly because of competition from the starting of tram services, the station was never a success and in August 1890, the LBSCR was given powers to close the line. The site of the station and land was sold to the Croydon Corporation who erected a replacement town hall and public gardens on the site.

In the year 1881, a grisly life or death struggle took place in a train as it sped through the Surrey countryside. In fact, were it not for the sharp eyes of a woman in a cottage not far from the railway line at Horley, a case of murder might well have been difficult to prove. It was by chance she looked out of her window to see two men struggling in a compartment of a passing train.

Merstham station c1910. An earlier site in 1841 was considered for use as a junction for trains to Brighton and also SER trains to Dover. (Lens of Sutton)

It was apparently a protracted struggle and by the time the train reached Balcombe tunnel, the victim's body had been bundled out onto the track. At Preston Park a young man staggered from a compartment, covered in blood, saying he had been attacked and robbed. He was taken to Brighton Police Station where it was thought he had attempted suicide.

He returned home to Wallington escorted by a detective (named Holmes!) who saw him to his house to change his clothes. But the young man, whose name was Lefroy, left quickly by a back door. Meanwhile the victim had been found to be Frederick Gold, a 60 year old stockbroker. By now evidence was being collected from the Horley witness and this, with other information, indicated that Lefroy was the murderer. Lefroy was eventually arrested in Stepney by someone claiming a £100 reward and he was found guilty and hanged on November 29th 1881.

Horley station was originally planned to be built on a far more extensive scale than others south of Croydon. It was decided that its position half way between London and Brighton and its siting on a flat terrain would be ideal for building carriage sheds and engine workshops. Water could be drawn from the nearby river Mole and the proposed location was to be over a considerable area immediately west of the original station.

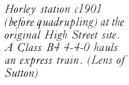

Horley station c1901 (before quadrupling) at the original High Street site. A Class B4 4-4-0 hauls an express train. (Lens of Sutton)

The station was first built north of today's site with an entrance from the present High Street. A level crossing existed immediately to the north of the station and a second was built to the south where Victoria Road now crosses the line. Even though plans to build the workshops were dropped, quite a lot of work was carried out there. In the period 1884 to 1903, many aging locomotives were scrapped in a siding on the up side. In 1949 the 'scrapyard' opened up again for a few years.

Chapter 3

'ATMOSPHERIC' TRAINS
THAT RAN ON AIR!

In October 1845, nearly four years after steam trains had commenced services on the London to Brighton line, trials of 'atmospheric trains' began between Forest Hill and Croydon. Had they proved successful then traction methods for many years to come could have been revolutionised. The system claimed to be clean, fast and almost noiseless. Speeds of over 60 mph were claimed and, in a later run, 70 mph was claimed with a six vehicle train. For a time many considered that steam trains would be phased out!

In June 1827, a meeting had been held in Brighton where support was given to an atmospheric line from London to Brighton for 'the conveyance of passengers between Brighton and the Metropolis' and an extension to Shoreham Harbour 'for the transit of goods'. A company called the 'London, Brighton and Shoreham Pneumatic Conveyance Co.' was formed and annual profits were anticipated at 10%. Unfortunately for the promoters, lack of finance forced them to drop the idea.

In 1838 a similar patent granted Samuel Clegg (previously a gas engineer) and Jacob and Joseph Samuda (ship-builders) had led to practical results. In essence the idea was that a train would literally run on air, being a combination of a partial vacuum and atmospheric pressure. The system eliminated the need for locomotives but required the laying of a continuous iron pipe between the rails. Stationary engines by the trackside pumped the air from the pipe which had a continuous slot in it covered by a leather flap hinged on one side but able to lift on the other.

The leading carriage had a rod fitted underneath which carried a piston inside the pipe. Two wheels in front of the attachment lifted the flap in front of the rod and a small wheel behind sealed it again. It was the vacuum ahead of the piston and the atmospheric pressure behind it that propelled the train.

Disadvantages were many. It was expected that the vacuum would more or less cease about the time the train reached its next stopping point and a handbrake would not be necessary to bring it to a halt, but this did not always happen. Reversing was not easily possible since the piston only moved forward. Because of this trains frequently had to be moved – either manually or by a horse with a tow-rope or even on occasions by the unfortunate 3rd class passengers! Alternatively the track had to be built on an incline.

When reversing became a necessity at the end of a line it was quite a complicated business. The piston assembly had to be

Originally part of an engine-house used with the Atmospheric trains at West Croydon, the building was moved to Surrey Street, Croydon, in 1851 where it became a pumping house for local main water supply. (Author)

unbolted from the piston carriage with the latter turned around and the piston and its driving arm refixed to the train. Further problems appeared to be that a satisfactory system of constructing points had not been worked out and also level crossings were difficult because of the pipe between the rails.

Advantages also existed, claimed the inventors. These included reduced permanent way costs, no smoke or dirt and also high speeds were possible. Elimination of collisions was a factor since only one train could be between pumping stations at any one time.

Trials began on the West London Railway in June 1840 in the Kensington area which were considered successful. In August 1840 the idea was put to the London & Croydon Railway but no immediate decision was made. Meantime the Irish Government granted a loan of £25,000 to the Dublin & Kingstown Railway for an experimental line to be built between Kingstown and Dalkey. This proved successful, operating over a single track nearly two miles long. Regular services commenced on August 18th 1843 lasting some twelve years.

The London & Croydon Railway's shareholders now showed interest in the idea and a decision was made on March 7th 1844 that an independent atmospheric line should be built from London to Croydon. Parliamentary approval was given in August 1844.

Stage one of the construction was to be from West Croydon to the Dartmouth Arms (now Forest Hill). Stages two and three proposed a line to New Cross and London Bridge and finally stage four was planned to Sutton and Epsom from West Croydon. A separate track, to be built on the down side between Forest Hill and Norwood, was considered necessary so as not to impede the longer distance services of the London & Brighton Railway (L&BR) and the South Eastern Railway (SER). Between Norwood and West Croydon the atmospheric trains had to

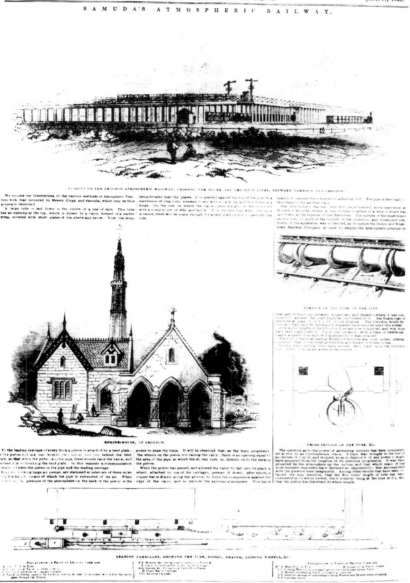

Details of the Atmospheric railway from an October 1845 edition of The Illustrated London News. *The top picture shows the 'flying junction' south of the* Jolly Sailor *(now Norwood Junction) – the first of its kind in the world. Part of the engine house, previously at West Croydon, can be seen today at Surrey Street's water works. (by courtesy of the National Railway Museum, York)*

cross the ordinary tracks and because of this the first ever fly-over bridge in the world was built. The length was about 700 yards and it was a timber construction. It was later replaced by an embankment which still remains in evidence today.

The Epsom branch was initially sponsored by an independent company although the L&CR originally had ambitious ideas that atmospheric trains would eventually reach Portsmouth! Between Croydon and Epsom plans were made for a single track with a crossing loop at Carshalton (renamed Wallington in 1868) thus allowing a regular hourly service. How the promoters would have overcome the points problem does not appear to have been recorded. Other intermediate stations planned included Sutton, Cheam and Ewell (now Ewell East). The station at Epsom was to be the one later used by the LBSCR and closed by the Southern Railway in 1929 (see Chapter 10).

Pumping stations on the initial stretch were at Forest Hill, Norwood Junction and Croydon. The stations were given 'architectural' treatment to make them less unsightly and the final result of the Norwood Engine House resembled more a steep-roofed church and steeple than an engine house and chimney. The 'stations' were operated by pairs of single cylinder beam engines fired by a mixture of coal and coke.

By late summer 1845 the first trial between Forest Hill and Croydon took place. Speeds over 60 mph were claimed and a five mile run without renewed use of a pumping station. In a later run, 70 mph was claimed with a six vehicle train.

Optimism was soon dashed as mechanical failures started to occur and in some cases engine crankshafts broke. Public opening was delayed. Despite the earlier successful trials, 1845 proved a disappointing year and it worsened when, in November of that year, one of the Samuda brothers, Jacob, was killed by an accident to one of his steamships on the Thames.

Troubles persisted with work on the Croydon to Epsom line suffering delays over difficulties in acquiring certain areas of land. Also the 'steeple' on the Croydon engine house had to be removed as it had become unsafe due to heavy vibration. Expenditure on the engine houses was continually increasing. Eventu-

Pipes from the Atmospheric railway dug out in 1933 not far from West Croydon station (by courtesy of the National Railway Museum, York).

ally a public opening was fixed for January 19th 1846, but when the day came two engines broke down and the atmospheric system had to suffer the indignity of having steam locomotives to assist. The service was withdrawn.

By Easter 1846 the weather took a hand in worsening matters

with the period proving the start of a very hot summer. The flap at the top of the tube (through which the arm projected) became ineffective because the heat melted the mixture of beeswax and tallow intended to seal the area. As luck would have it, the winter that followed was a bitter one. Temperatures as low as -11 degrees Centigrade (12 degrees F) were recorded causing the leather of the valves to crack which caused further leakages.

All this required additional pumping. Further complications arose when rubbish was drawn into the pipe and then sucked to pumping stations. There are stories that even rats were drawn into the system! Air valves were choked and train workings deteriorated further. Although trains resumed publicly in July 1846, there remained instances of failure to stop at stations and of buffer collisions at Croydon when rails were greasy.

The end came nearer when in July 1846 the London & Croydon Railway amalgamated with the Brighton company to become the London, Brighton & South Coast Railway (LBSCR). The new company became increasingly disillusioned about atmospheric trains and later in the year the board asked Joseph Samuda if he would like to work the trains for a period on a contract basis. Samuda, still convinced that his idea had a future, experimented with a trial run from New Cross to Croydon – with no intermediate stops – to convince any doubters. The train, a piston carriage and three vehicles with a total weight of over 16 tons, reached Croydon in twelve and a half minutes giving an average speed from start to stop of 36 mph.

But this was not enough to win overall support and the case for abandoning the system was strengthened following a serious fire at West Croydon in September 1846 which destroyed the atmospheric shed and ten carriages. The directors decided to investigate the project's finances and by the end of the year discovered that as much as £228,290 had been invested in the New Cross to Croydon line and £186,169 in the Epsom branch.

By March 1847 the LBSCR, not surprisingly, gave up the system altogether. The atmospheric railway had lasted officially just over a year during which time a plan to extend from New Cross to London Bridge had been shelved and work already carried out on the stretch from West Croydon to Epsom had been abandoned. The steam locomotives had won their day.

The engines, atmospheric tubes and all other equipment were offered for sale but there were no buyers. Finally much of the gear was auctioned fetching minimum scrap value only. Only the engine house at Croydon North End aroused interest. On 21st May 1850, the Croydon Local Board of Health, requiring a new pumping station for main water supply, approached the LBSCR with an offer of £250. This was accepted and at the end of the year the building was removed to a new location in Surrey Street, where despite many alterations and additions, it remains to this day. The Forest Hill engine survived until 1944 when it was hit by a flying bomb.

Chapter 4

THE 'OVERHEAD' ELECTRICS

It is easy today to take the 'third rail' electric trains for granted but there was a period when working with overhead cables was used in parts of Surrey. Such a service was extended from London to Coulsdon North and to Sutton on April 1st 1925, but the idea lasted only four and a half years. On Sunday, September 22nd 1929, the last AC 'overhead' electric train left Victoria and stock was converted to the now familiar DC traction.

As early as 1901 an idea for a monorail system was put forward for an independent electric railway from London to Brighton. The scheme was originally based on the Behr Monorail principle similar to a project previously authorised between Liverpool and Manchester although it was soon agreed it should be a more conventional high-speed line.

A terminus was planned at Lupus Street in the Pimlico area of London and at Brighton a station was to be considered at the Metropole. Between Cane Hill and Redhill a 3½ mile tunnel would accommodate trains under the North Downs. There would be no stations along the route but loops of some length through important areas, such as Croydon, would be incorporated to allow through or separate trains. It was reckoned the journey would take 32 minutes at a cost of 5/-d (25p) return first class!

Because a rival monorail scheme, backed by a London syndicate, was being considered and since Brighton Council were showing no interest in any such systems, the original ideas were changed considerably. Tracks were now planned from Waterloo to Croydon on a continuous viaduct with 'a roadway for vehicular traffic underneath' and an elevated terminus would be built at Furze Hill in Brighton with passenger approach by hydraulic lifts. Stations would be sited at Croydon, Redhill, Horley and Haywards Heath. In addition the cost had escalated – from an estimated £6m to £9m – and the journey time increased to 40 minutes.

Brighton's feelings about such plans were hardening. Certain elements of Brighton's society were against the idea for fear it would encourage 'large numbers of day trippers'. By the time the Bill for the project, submitted by the London & Brighton Electric Railway, reached Parliament, it was rejected.

The following year there was another proposal on the Behr system but this time using LBSCR property. It was of course rejected by the railway company's directors and the Bill was withdrawn. But the challenge remained for the LBSCR who felt some counter-action was necessary. They also felt spurred to greater effort by a report in the *The Times* which had expressed dismay over their London to Brighton line describing it as a 'crawl to the South'.

The fastest train on the LBSCR timetable was then the 5 pm from London Bridge which reached Brighton in 1 hour 5 minutes. On Sunday, July 26th 1903, a train left Victoria comprising three Pullman cars and a brake van hauled by the B4 class Holyrood to cover the 50 miles 73 chains in 48 minutes 41 seconds. The average speed was 63.4 mph with the maximum of 90 mph being attained near Horley. The return journey took 50 minutes 21 seconds. Thus the company considered they had not only showed the capacity of their steam trains but also demonstrated their effectiveness against the possibility of electric traction.

An 'unusual' idea was put forward in November 1905, when a concern suggested a roadway from Croydon to Patcham (north of Brighton) to carry vehicular traffic. It was to be known as a 'motor-way' but the Bill was withdrawn in February 1906. Clearly the idea was well before its time!

Despite the LBSCR's reluctance to consider electric trains, it was inevitable that they should come about. With quadrupling on sections of the Brighton line in hand, the company conceded that this would give them 'two tracks for the latest novelties in traction . . .' Ultimately it was falling receipts on the South London surburban lines and also increasing competition from London's trams that forced the situation, since by now the LBSCR was losing business at an alarming rate. It was eventually accepted that the only alternative to the drastic step of closing uneconomic routes was electrification. Operating costs would be reduced and, with greater acceleration, more trains could be run.

A Billinton C2 Class 0-6-0 No. 542 passed under 'overhead electric' cables at South Croydon c1925. (Lens of Sutton)

LBSCR D1 tank No. 298 propels a single coach at West Croydon under electric cables c1925. (Lens of Sutton)

By January 1909, electric trains were being run between Battersea Park and East Brixton. Work was carried out by Robert Blackwell and Co. with materials coming from the All-gemeine Elektricitats Gesellschaft – known as AEG of Berlin. Soon electric trains were extended to Peckham Rye and, by December 1909, a line from London Bridge to Victoria had its public opening. The trains were running on a 6,700 volt 25 Hz AC overhead wire system. Success was immediate. The trains proved, as expected, more efficient than their steam counterparts and traffic increased. They became known as the 'Elevated Electrics' but were soon referred to as just 'The Overhead'.

By May 12th 1911, similar trains reached Crystal Palace from Victoria via Balham. The line was opened in time for the Festival of Empire held at Crystal Palace and opened on that date by King George V. Work on the Tulse Hill line was completed in the same year although this section was never brought into regular use. Soon lines with overhead cables extended to Norwood Junction and Selhurst. These latter two were brought into use earlier than expected to economise on the use of coal for locomotives – due to a coal strike early in 1912!

The three-coach units initially employed on the suburban routes were quickly withdrawn partly because there were too many first-class compartments. When two-coach units were introduced they proved immediately popular. The rolling stock used on the Coulsdon North and Sutton serviecs was of a different type. Instead of power bogies being fitted under the passenger-carrying coaches, separate motor vehicles were used and a typical formation would be a five-car unit with the motor unit third. Each motor van was fitted with four 250 hp single-phase motors

An 'overhead electric' en route to Sutton at Carshalton Beeches. The service opened officially on April 1 1925. (Lens of Sutton)

and often two five-car units would be run together to cater for peak traffic.

Future plans included electrification to East Croydon and Coulsdon North, West Croydon, Sutton and Cheam and another to Sutton via Mitcham Junction. Cheam had been included due to the inadequacy of sidings at Sutton plus the fact that Cheam was a fast growing residential suburb. But in 1914 the war came and all progress was halted. It was particularly affected because much of the project involved the use of German equipment.

Work was slow to pick up again after 1918. In 1921 plans were forwarded to electrify the Brighton line but there were no immediate results. The planned extensions to Coulsdon North and Sutton were started in 1922. Cable supports to Coulsdon North were built by 1923 but the catenaries and conductors were not finished until autumn 1924. When both services finally opened on April 1st 1925, Carshalton Beeches (formerly Beeches Halt) on the Sutton line was still being enlarged.

The 'overheads' lasted until 1929 by which time the Southern Railway decided that any further progress would be standardised on the 'third rail' low voltage DC system already proven elsewhere in the region. In addition it had been found that costs for the overhead equipment had been higher than anticipated. By September 1929, equipment had been converted and electric trains, on the system known today, reached Sutton and Coulsdon North from Victoria (a London Bridge – Coulsdon North service had begun earlier in June 1928). Such was their popularity that a new electric line was built on the third rail system from Wimbledon to Sutton and opened by 1930.

At the same time the Southern Railway announced a plan to

electrify the line from Coulsdon North to Brighton via Redhill and the Quarry line together with a branch to Reigate. The total cost including new stock and resignalling was estimated at approximately £2,700,000 but it was considered this would be more than offset by an anticipated increase in annual train mileage from just under 2 million to nearly 5 million.

Work began in 1931 with many signal boxes demolished under the new signalling system and a total of 285 new coaches were provided which included 38 Pullman cars. Electric trains reached Three Bridges on July 17th 1932, and from that date, Salfords Halt, originally built in October 1915 for the employees of the nearby Monotype Works, was brought into public service. The service to the coast was formally opened on 30th December the same year. An attraction of the new service was the hourly non-stop run from Victoria to Brighton which reached its destination in just the hour. During tests a run was completed in 46 minutes 43 seconds – almost two minutes faster than the LBSCR's 'Holyrood' in 1903!

Press reaction to the new trains was good. An article in *The Times* said the third class carriages were 'quite as comfortable as the first-class carriages on our most progressive lines in pre-war days'. The feature praised the trains for not belching 'stifling smoke . . . through Merstham Tunnel' and finished with some stern advice – hardly heeded today – 'After this foretaste of electric luxury let who will creep at their own and others' peril along the highway: sensible and self-regarding persons will stick to the train'.

By 1939 many lines had been converted and a new electric branch to Chessington South from Motspur Park had been completed. Plans to electrify the Oxted line had to be shelved when World War II broke out. Only now, nearly fifty years later, has the proposal reached fruition with the Sanderstead to East Grinstead link having opened in October 1987.

There is no doubt that the 'Southern Electric' service has proved highly successful but it also had its critics. With the third rail operation, adverse weather can quickly throw a whole section into chaos. When the electric services began, the railway authorities advertised, 'You won't need a timetable'. Perhaps when the conductor rail is coated with ice, they could well be right.

Chapter 5

SKIRMISHES AROUND GUILDFORD

When the first train steamed out of Guildford station destined for Woking at 7.30 am on May 5th 1845, there was free beer all round – despite the early hour – for the workmen who had built the line. It was an occasion of great celebration and the journey of just over six miles was completed in twelve minutes.

Guildford has been a meeting place of travellers throughout the centuries. Once an ancient market town and a centre of local agricultural life, it was also famous for its cloth making and as a stopping place for the Portsmouth coaches. It was not surprising that its importance grew when the railways arrived.

The Guildford Junction Company was authorised to build the short branch from Woking in 1844. Initially it was planned that the trains would be far from conventional, to be run on what was known as Prosser's system. The idea comprised engines and coaches using flangeless wooden wheels to be run on flat wooden track with additional guide wheels pressing at angles to the sides and the tops of the rails. When Prosser had patented his idea in 1844, he claimed that his locomotive had travelled about 3,000 miles during a period of two months without any repair necessary. One of the main features demonstrated was that under such circumstances a train could not derail.

In fact any mileage completed must have been during trial runs on Wimbledon Common where a circular test track of ten chains radius had been constructed including gradients of up to 1 in 50. Apparently a further trial line existed near Vauxhall Bridge where experiments were watched by numerous engineers.

The Guildford company successfully sought the support of the LSWR but the latter was far from happy with the Prosser system. The scheme would in any event have prevented through working of LSWR trains thus requiring an unnecessary change at Woking. Perhaps it was just as well for the future of railway history that the LSWR, when purchasing the line, insisted on conventional trains. At least for William Prosser, the LSWR purchase price for the Guildford Junction Company included a sum of £2,000 compensation.

However this was not quite the end of such a system. Apparently his idea – or something quite similar – was used in France in 1848 on a 25 mile line from Paris to Limours lasting over 40 years.

Further lines from Guildford were soon to follow. In 1849 a link to Farnham was established and in 1852 this was extended to become the Alton line. Both these areas were barley-growing districts and a heavy traffic of locally brewed ale was expected.

Hitherto some 145,000 barrels had been conveyed annually by road to Winchfield on the main Basingstoke–Woking line for conveyance to London. Further freight was expected from stone quarries near Alton, previously not exploited through transport difficulties.

The route today from Guildford to Alton takes a traveller through Wanborough, Ash and Aldershot to Farnham but the original line took a more south westerly direction through Ash Green and Tongham. These stations were closed for passenger traffic when electrification came in July 1937 and the stretch was finally abandoned in 1961. The line was not without its incidents. In 1862 a LSWR goods train went out of control down the gradient towards Guildford station to collide with a SER goods train. The enginemen managed to jump to safety before the impact. Five years later ten people were injured when a SER train was hit by another from Alton, due to a signalman's error.

At Ash Green there was an incident which set a pattern for the future. The intention was to detach a horse box and carriage from a Guildford to Southampton train so that a wagon which contained the furniture and effects of a transferred signalman could be added. As the train reversed to regain the horse box and carriage, the buffers were contacted but trouble with coupling caused the vehicles to jump the scotches (wooden structures swung across the line) allowing them to reverse down a gradient. Porters threw ballast on the line whilst the guard tried to scotch the wheels but in vain. Four passengers jumped to safety before a goods train was struck at Ash Junction. As a result of the accident, rear brake vans became a necessity on all trains in future on the line.

Ash Green station still remains today although it is now a

Guildford railway station c1910. The station opened on May 5 1845. (Lens of Sutton) private property. The route of the old line remains clearly visible from the nearby overbridge. Tongham station not far away has been demolished but some evidence of the old platform can be traced. The station building which once stood astride the platforms on the overbridge has gone.

During a visit by the author to Tongham in July 1987, a number of square stone blocks lying in the grass near the station site caused some excitement. No doubt found under the platform during demolition, local historians consider it likely they were originally spare stone sleepers from the CM&G days of earlier last century. Each block weighs about 5 cwt and some have been drilled, presumably to take the cast iron chairs necessary to secure the rails.

In 1849, the same year that Farnham was reached, a line was opened southwards from Guildford to Godalming being part of the LSWR's bid to reach Portsmouth. There had been other contenders in the field. These included the Brighton & Chichester company (later to become part of the LBSCR) who had applied for powers to extend westwards via Chichester and Havant. Another company, the Direct London & Portsmouth, with the support of the Croydon company, had sought powers to build a line from Epsom via Dorking and Godalming using atmospheric propulsion – a system currently being experimented upon by the Croydon company (chapter 3).

In the end only the Brighton & Chichester company's bill received assent and this was agreed in August 1845. Meantime the LSWR, which still considered its Bishopstoke (later Eastleigh)–Gosport route to Portsmouth quite adequate, signed an agreement with the Brighton company. This included a requirement that the two companies would support a further

The entrance to Guildford station July 1987. The ornate covered-way at the entrance has gone but numerous buildings remain. (Author)

Guildford station in the days of steam around 1909 when tracks left the junction in six different directions. (Pamlin Prints)

project, the Guildford, Chichester & Portsmouth with a proposed route via Godalming, Haslemere and Midhurst, to compete against the Direct atmospheric line. The agreement lasted only until the Croydon and Brighton companies amalgamated to become the LBSCR which in turn now supported the Direct scheme.

Eventually the Direct London & Portsmouth line was authorised, provided that Portsmouth remained a station jointly owned by all three companies and also that conventional trains were used – following the failure of the atmospheric system. Despite the go-ahead, no work was ever carried out on the Direct line due to financial difficulties and the virtual end of the 'railway mania' period. On June 14th 1847, LBSCR trains reached Portsmouth via Chichester but this did not satisfy London travellers who still considered that a shorter and direct route should be available. Neither the LSWR nor the LBSCR were interested in such a plan, since less miles meant less fares collected. So the idea was taken up by the Portsmouth Railway Company which received Parliamentary approval to build a line from Havant to Godalming (already reached from Guildford) in 1853. The intention was that the Portsmouth company should build a 'contractor's line' with the idea of selling or leasing when completed to any interested party.

At this stage a further complication came about with the South Eastern Railway receiving approval for a spur to be built from Shalford from their Redhill–Guildford line (completed in 1849) to join the existing line to Godalming. The SER claimed it would not work Portsmouth Railway lines because of an agreement with the LBSCR to respect territories, but with the possibility of a through SER route from Redhill to Portsmouth, the LSWR felt

compelled to lease the new line. To become known as the Portsmouth Direct Line, this included running powers over LBSCR track from Havant to Portcreek Junction north of Portsmouth and it was this agreement which gave rise to the 'battle' that was to follow.

Guildford station in July 1987. Apart from electrification, little appears changed since the turn of the century. To the left are two diesel units (ex-Western Region stock) providing a Gatwick Airport–Reading service. (Author)

In his book, *A Regional History of the Railways – Southern England* H.P. White describes the events. The LBSCR, not unexpectedly, objected to this route, 20 miles less than their own, part of which shared their metals. Arbitration failed and the LSWR, now impatient to use its new line already twelve months completed, announced that a goods train would use the Havant – Portcreek Junction section of December 28th 1858, prior to commencement of a regular passenger service four days later.

On the day, the 'goods train' was manned by almost one hundred platelayers and other robust employees of the LSWR. On arrival at Havant, three hours earlier than announced, it was found the 'Brighton' people were quite prepared. The points had been removed and an engine had been left on the crossing during the night. The points were soon relaid and the engine forcibly seized, but by this time the 'enemy' had mustered its forces and lifted a rail on the main line blocking any LSWR escape. A serious fight appeared imminent but it was averted and, after two hours, the LSWR retreated back to Guildford.

The passenger service from Guildford to Portsmouth began as announced but travellers were compelled to travel by bus from Havant. Legal action followed and eventually an injunction was served on the Brighton company restraining it from interference with through LSWR running. A fares war followed at considerable loss to both companies before a final agreement was reached. The disputed section became joint property in 1860.

The remains of Ash Green station platform which closed to passengers in July 1937. (Lens of Sutton)

Tongham station building c1910, on the original line from Guildford to Alton. (Lens of Sutton)

Guildford continued to grow in importance as a railway junction. The SER line from Redhill and Dorking, opened in 1849, linked with GWR lines at Reading, being part of an ambitious scheme to reach the Channel ports from the Midlands and the West. Initially the connection was useless since the GWR at that time operated a wider gauge but eventually an Act of July 1854 rectified this anomaly. In 1865 LBSCR trains reached Guildford from Horsham (Chapter 13) and twenty years later trains reached Guildford from Hampton Court Junction (on the main Woking line) along the New Guildford Line via Cobham.

Immediately south of Guildford station, St Catherine's tunnel and Chalk tunnel are located. These were obviously negotiated with alarm in earlier times particularly since in 1876 the northern end of Chalk tunnel had collapsed. Apparently a train passing through stopped in such good time that a passenger gave over £9 for the driver, fireman and other staff to share! There was trouble too in St Catherine's tunnel when the crown collapsed in 1895. An empty train was trapped without injury to staff and an hour later was buried by another fall. It was nine days before single-line working was possible.

Guildford station dates from a reconstruction in the 1880s which included seven facing platforms and a short bay. It also had a coal stage, loading docks, a goods shed, stables and a corn store. To the south was the familiar 'Roundhouse' locomotive shed which survived until the demise of steam. A subsequent historic event for Guildford station was the arrival of electric

Stones each weighing about 5 cwt with some bearing drilling holes near the site of Tongham station photographed by the author in July 1987. Their presence remains a mystery since when the line was opened by the LSWR in 1849, wooden sleepers were used. It is thought possible they originally came from the Croydon, Merstham and Godstone Railway. (Author)

trains in July 1925, an event that was loudly proclaimed by the Town Crier!

At its height, Guildford handled trains in six different directions. Although spacious, it was considered to be awkwardly laid out and at one time, LSWR notices were displayed advising passengers not to board a train before ascertaining its direction. Perhaps some passengers today may experience the same feeling!

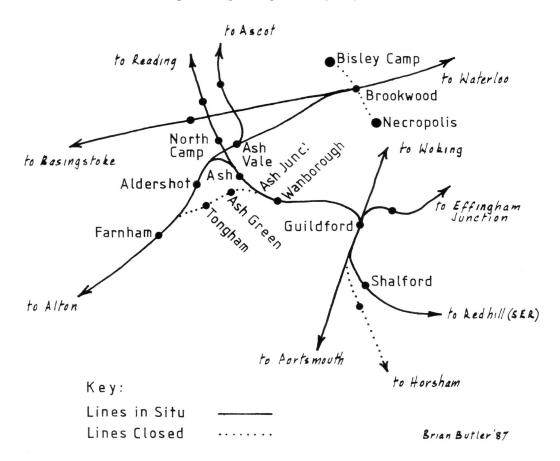

Key:

Lines in Situ ————

Lines Closed ·······

Brian Butler '87

Chapter 6

AN SER LINE ACROSS SURREY –
READING TO REDHILL

The Reading, Guildford & Reigate Company was incorporated in 1846 to build a line nearly 46 miles long from Reigate (later called Redhill) to Reading on the main GWR line to the West Country. The SER was very willing to support such an enterprise, seeing it as a through link from the West to the Channel ports. The route was quite a complicated one running south-east from Reading to Farnborough, then on to Ash Junction where it joined the LSWR branch from Alton. From Ash Junction through Guildford to Shalford Junction, running powers over LSWR lines were agreed and from Shalford the route was back on its own metals following the southern slopes of the North Downs to Reigate.

The line took a long time to build and was considered to be poorly constructed. It had been approved by Acts of 1846 and 1847 with a further Act dated 1849 to cover the company's use of LSWR metals from Ash to Shalford Junction. First lines to open were on July 4th 1849, from Reigate to Dorking and Reading to Farnborough. In the following month, trains reached Shalford from Dorking, and Guildford from Farnborough, but it was not until 15 October that the line was completed. Whilst waiting for the Shalford–Guildford stretch to open, passengers had to be content with a horse-bus connection.

In 1852 the SER decided to buy the line, a decision which

A Southern Railway ex LSWR Drummond T9 at Ash station in the late 1920s with a class M7 in the bay on the left. (Lens of Sutton)

antagonised many shareholders who were unhappy about the high price offered and who had doubts about the viability of the route in general. The SER Chairman had argued that the line served as an invaluable link between the GWR and the south-east coast ports, yet rather neglecting the fact that, at that time, there was no continuation beyond Reading because of the GWR broad-gauge track. Despite the fact that a 'Regulation of Gauge Act' had been introduced in August 1846, the situation at Reading was not regularised until 1858, some twelve years later.

The line could have assumed greater importance when, in 1859, a company called the Portsmouth Railway, formed in 1853, completed a line between Guildford and Portsmouth via Godalming and Havant. A link between Godalming and Shalford (on the new SER line) was given approval which would allow Portsmouth trains to reach London via Reigate on a route 12 miles shorter than the LBSCR route to the capital via Brighton. Work started on a curve to join the two lines and a wooden trestle bridge was built over the river Wey. Even a building was constructed for an intended station at Peasmarsh. However the SER decided to honour an agreement with the LBSCR not to 'poach' in another territory and the spur was removed before completion. Had it remained, Shalford could perhaps have become an important railway junction. It was of course this SER decision which resulted in LSWR trains adopting the 'Portsmouth Direct' route.

Shalford station could have been an important junction had a spur to the Portsmouth line been completed! (Lens of Sutton)

Earlier in 1854 the Government had financed the building of army camps near a small village called Aldershot and by 1855, North and South Camps were officially opened by Queen Victoria. This of course encouraged some traffic on the otherwise

quiet SER line and by 1858 a station on the Reading line was
opened at North Camp. The first station built was on the north
side of the level crossing but several years later the present long,
low station buildings were constructed on the south side where
there were ample sidings. Today the station has kept its promi-
nence with Gatwick–Reading trains calling there as well as the
Tonbridge diesel multiple units (DMUs). In addition there is
currently a two-siding oil depot but a neglected and rusting
up-siding remains as a memory of the past.

*A 'not very clean'
Drummond T9
(ex-LSWR) locomotive at
Betchworth station around
the end of World War II.
(Lens of Sutton)*

Ash station opened in August 1849, when the line began, but
Wanborough opened much later in September 1891, as a station
on the now-closed Tongham line. Between Ash and Wanborough
the earthworks from the old Tongham line can still be deter-
mined. An unusual feature concerning Wanborough station is an
agreement that platform tickets should never be sold!

Beyond Guildford, Shalford station had a complex goods yard
plus a narrow-gauge tramway serving a timber yard. There was a
small loco-shed and, until recently, a large depot for making up
trackwork. Truly the makings of an important junction had that
spur to the Portsmouth line been built. On a recent journey by
the author, the diesel train stopped for only a few seconds at
Shalford with no passengers getting on or off. Now permanently
unstaffed, today's station is reduced to two short staggered
platforms each with a metal shelter. What a sad decline.

After Shalford came Chilworth and Albury, now called simply
Chilworth. Here the railway picks up the course of the Tilling
Bourne with Chilworth being another unmanned stop. The
original gabled and decorated station house is now let out for
private use. In his book *Railways of the Southern Region*, Geoffrey

The remains of an office at Betchworth Quarry in 1986 where numerous sidings (using three different gauges!) once existed. (Author)

Body writes that in the old signal box, it was not unknown for the signalman to find a snake nestling under the floorboards! And the barrier crossing is now CCTV operated with the old gates now in use on the Dart Valley Railway.

Gomshall station opened with the line and was previously known as Gomshall and Shere – apparently earlier spelled as Sheire. Like other stations along the line it had a large goods siding. There was also a branch to a nearby sandpit – later used as a caravan park. Dorking came next, renamed Dorking Town in 1923, with Deepdene only half a mile further east. Deepdene opened in February 1851, as 'Box Hill and Leatherhead Road' to be renamed Box Hill in the same year. In 1923 it acquired its present name.

Nearby Deepdene Hotel achieved fame in the last war when the Southern Railway used it for its wartime headquarters. It was there that, day and night, throughout hostilities, experts planned the movement of special trains and equipment for the forces with particular emphasis on pre-D Day activities. The author writes this paragraph with some pride for his father, Victor Oppitz, was a member of the railway staff at Deepdene and was closely involved with troop movements, yet never once breathed a word of his work.

At one time a single line spur linked the SER line between Deepdene and Betchworth to the LBSCR route from Leatherhead to Epsom. As far as is known it was used only once for a race-special from Hastings to Epsom. The spur was lifted in 1926 but relaid as a temporary measure during wartime in 1941.

Betchworth retains its original 1849 gabled style building on the down side although now somewhat run-down. The station was noted for its extensive railway system serving the lime works to the north. There were three gauges, standard, 3 ft 2¼ ins and 1 ft 6 ins. Today they have all gone but a derelict office near the entrance remains. The 3 ft 2¼ ins quarry line closed in 1959 but the locomotives 0-4-OT 'Townsend Hook' and 'William Finlay' (Fletcher and Jennings, 1880) were independently acquired for preservation in 1960. After various locations they were united again recently at Amberley Chalk Pits Museum near Arundel in West Sussex where restoration of the engines is taking place. A further locomotive, 0-4-OT standard gauge 'Baxter' (Fletcher and Jennings, 1877), was delivered in 1960 to the Bluebell Railway at Sheffield Park.

Reigate station opened as 'Reigate Town' (see chapter 7) when the line began. The tall chimneyed and multi-gabled buildings on the down side are original. When electrification came to the Brighton line in 1932, the short section to Reigate was included whereupon many semi-fast trains to London included four coaches from Three Bridges and four from Reigate joining at Redhill's platform 2. At one time it was intended to build a spur at Redhill to give through running from Reading to Brighton and it was no doubt inter-company rivalry that ensured that this did not happen.

The Redhill to Reading section remains a vital link in a route to bypass London. Apart from regular services, an hourly service of diesel units (ex Western Region stock) is provided today between Gatwick Airport and Reading. Some of these are semi-fast, completing the journey in less than 1½ hours. Had that spur been built at Redhill they could be even quicker, avoiding that Redhill reversal.

Steam and electric join forces at Reigate station in the early 1950s. (Lens of Sutton)

Chapter 7

AN SER LINE ACROSS SURREY –
REDHILL TO TONBRIDGE

When Parliament sanctioned a line from London to Brighton in 1837, MPs considered, with total lack of foresight, that one rail entrance into London from the south was sufficient. Because of this the SER was obliged to accept that any major route they planned to the east should commence at Reigate (later known as Redhill) with part of the remaining route from London to be shared with the rival London and Brighton Railway. Under such circumstances a line from Reigate to Tonbridge was built eventually reaching Dover in February 1844.

The first 'Reigate' station opened on the Brighton line (just north of Earlswood) in July 1841, by which time L&BR trains had reached Haywards Heath. The Redhill (SER) station on the Tonbridge line (then spelled Tunbridge) opened less than a year later in May 1842. The two 'Redhill' stations were badly sited, being at each end of Hooley Lane – then a muddy ill-lit road. Despite frequent complaints from travellers, the inconvenience continued for two years by which time a joint station had been built at the present site, where the lines separated. The name remained 'Reigate' until 1849 when the SER opened a line westwards to Dorking and the present Reigate station (then called Reigate Town) came into being. The confusion was regularised when the original Reigate became Redhill.

The present station at Redhill was rebuilt in 1858 on the site of the earlier 1844 station with part of the original buildings remaining at the south end, down side. Redhill has been 'rebuilt' many

Looking northwards towards Redhill Junction (known as Redhill since 1929) c1910 where tracks left the main line to Tonbridge to the east and Reading to the west. (Lens of Sutton)

44

times with the last major change taking place in 1933. Many considered the station had been a 'nightmare' to work in busier times. In earlier days during holiday periods there were constant arrivals and departures including GWR trains splitting into different portions.

In May 1868, the SER's new main line to Tonbridge via Sevenoaks was opened which of course reduced the company's dependence on the Redhill route. Although fewer trains now ran via Redhill (SER) to the Kent coast, the route continued to play an important role over the years to come. In 1884 a double-track spur was built connecting the SER cross-country route to the newly opened Oxted line (joint LBSCR/SER owned) to allow trains from the Brighton line via Croydon to reach Tonbridge and beyond. When the Mid-Kent line opened in 1885 linking Woodside with Selsdon, SER trains were also given a through facility. Although the spur was removed in the 1960s it had served a useful purpose, not only for SER local services but also for excursion and goods trains from London to the Kent coast.

In the years that followed the line settled to a quiet existence. Apart from its growing use for cross-country services to the rapidly extending holiday resorts, it was perhaps not until the First World War that any changes were seen. Much of the traffic then comprised troop or hospital trains in addition to supplies being moved to the Channel ports.

After the war the railway remained run down and it did not really recover until after 'grouping' in 1923 when the Southern Railway was formed. This was also a time when the route served a new purpose. From 1920, the Redhill–Tonbridge line was followed by pilots of the new air service from London to Paris since the navigational aids of the day were not sufficiently reliable. To assist pilots, the names of Redhill and Tonbridge were painted in large letters on the station roofs to guide the planes back to the airport.

The east or 'down' side of Redhill station c1910 opened as 'Reigate' in 1844. (Lens of Sutton)

No doubt the line saw 'its finest hour' at the time of Dunkirk from May 27th to June 4th 1940. During that period there were no less than 565 special trains from the various ports all running to Redhill with many on to Reading. All regular services were stopped for the period and troop trains ran as and when they were required.

After the war, with the return of petrol, many passengers were lost to road traffic. Instead a commuter service to London gradually built up with many travellers coming from Nutfield and Godstone. Also due to the inadequacy of the nearby Oxted line, many more were coming from Edenbridge in Kent where there was a choice of station and route. With the end of steam now in sight, the future of the line became uncertain although somehow it managed to escape the Beeching axe. Possibly future military considerations or even the long promised Channel Tunnel secured the line's future, now dutifully served by ex-Western Region diesel trains built at Swindon in the early 1960s. In 1969 BR Southern Region planned to electrify many lines still worked by diesel including the Tonbridge–Redhill route. A BR representative said in February 1987 that plans were still in hand but, 'due to continually changing circumstances, such as the Channel Tunnel, no commitment could yet be given'. BR recognised however that the present diesels could not last indefinitely and it would not be too long before new diesel trains would have to be provided anyway.

An hourly stopping service runs at present along the route with fewer trains on Sundays. Any traveller transferring from the London to Brighton trains at Redhill would surely notice the difference. The trains do not have quite the same standard of

BR No. 31890 U1 Class at Leigh Halt on the Tonbridge–Redhill line in the late 1950s. (Lens of Sutton)

comfort and they appear less hurried. When the window is open in the summer, the smell of diesel fumes is certainly noticeable. Frequently the train will stop only briefly at a deserted platform before 'revving' again on its way.

At Godstone the platforms were built slightly staggered probably due to a nearby embankment. The station was opened with the line in May 1842, but during its time it acquired a modern (1914) building on the down side. Standing some three miles south of Godstone village, it was no doubt responsible for the smaller village that sprang up around it called South Godstone. Today the station's sidings have gone and the buildings have been replaced by unattractive shelters.

Between Godstone and Nutfield lies the 1326 yard Bletchingley Tunnel. During the Second World War there was a Home Guard post at the eastern end and it is said that on occasions drivers of goods trains would slow down and, on seeing a board held up bearing the word 'Coal', they would drop off a few lumps to keep the Home Guard's brazier going!

Nutfield opened later in 1883 being a more modern style than many stations. Again sidings existed including a long one to a chemical works put in over forty years ago where tank wagons were worked by Southern Railway locomotives.

In 1973 a Government grant of £610,000 was made towards the cost of the service and the railway authorities responded by encouraging travel with 'discount vouchers'. Some 150,000 of these were issued to encourage local people to use their line. But despite its current lack of patronage, the Redhill–Tonbridge route does not appear to be in any danger of closure – certainly not with the renewed possibility of a Channel Tunnel in the foreseeable future.

In the early days of the SER, whistle signals from locomotives were also used to inform pointsmen or signalmen of a train's direction. At Redhill, non-stop down trains whistled once if bound for Tonbridge, twice for Brighton and three times for Reading. How the staff in the Computer Room at the new BR Three Bridges Signalling Centre would shudder at such a thought today!

Lines separate to Tonbridge, Brighton and Guildford south of Redhill station. (Author)

Chapter 8

BROOKWOOD – A CEMETERY AND AN ARMY CAMP

The Brookwood Necropolis Railway, a short branch line off the LSWR main line between Woking and Farnborough, served an extensive cemetery and was certainly one of the more unusual branch lines. There were two stations on the ¾ mile single track line and it seemed that the final destination (in the earthly sense) depended upon one's faith since the North station was built for Non-Conformists and Roman Catholics and the South station for Anglicans!

It was probably the cholera epidemic of 1848/9 which had caused nearly 15,000 deaths in London alone that brought about this vast cemetery of nearly 2,200 acres in the Surrey countryside. The London Necropolis Company (LNC) was incorporated in 1852 and the scheme established in 1854 after numerous delays. In London a private terminus was built off York Street, near Waterloo.

Train services began their sober duties in November 1854 conveying the mourners and their deceased from London to Necropolis. Initially the railway company did well, gaining not only from the journey to the cemetery but also from subsequent visits by relatives. The trains consisted of normal coaches for the mourners and special hearse vans for the coffins. Charges for the conveyance of corpses were apparently high.

On arrival at Brookwood, the train was backed into a siding parallel to the down local line, after which it was propelled to the

Brookwood Necropolis North station. The track curves away into the distance to join the run-round loop adjacent to the main Woking line. (Lens of Sutton)

cemetery under the guard's supervision. North station was after only a quarter of a mile and the terminus at South station was half a mile further on. In each instance the brick-faced platforms were lowered half-way along their length to facilitate the unloading of the coffins.

In June 1863, the LSWR acceded to requests from local inhabitants and the LNC for a new station on the main line to be provided near the cemetery. Hitherto the nearest main line stop had been at Woking nearly four miles away. When Brookwood (Necropolis) opened on June 1st 1864, the land had been provided by the LNC who also built the approach roads and the station-master's house.

Brookwood station was enlarged in 1890 but when main-line quadrupling was carried out from Woking to Basingstoke during 1898/1902, the down platform was demolished to make way for the new tracks. A new platform was built on the cemetery side and there were extensions to buildings on the up platform.

Meantime in London, the site of the original York Street station was needed by the LSWR for necessary widening of tracks into Waterloo and by an agreement dated May 1899, the LSWR accepted the cost to construct a new Necropolis station and offices. The new terminus was opened in February 1902, and was situated at 121 Westminster Bridge Road, just south of Waterloo station. A tall four-storey building housed the LNC offices at the bottom of which was an impressive archway leading to the drive which passed into the station.

The Necropolis branch line came to a sudden end on the night

The remains of Necropolis North station, July 1987. The track was removed in the early 1950s and the station buildings demolished some ten years later. (Author)

of April 16th 1941, when high explosive bombs fell in the Westminster Bridge Road station sidings. Not only was the Necropolis train damaged but also much of the station and buildings. Nothing could be done to restore the service until after the end of the war when soon after May 1947, the LNC offices were transferred to Brookwood. The decision not to restore the Necropolis train service at that time seemed logical since the motor-hearse had now taken its place.

By 1953 the branch line track had been removed and in the 1960s the North station was demolished. South station continued as a refreshment room until 1967. After closure it became a store but on September 22nd 1972, half the building was destroyed by fire apparently caused by vandals. When the remainder of the building was demolished later, a chapter in history had come to an end and for many years since that time, only the outlines of the two platforms have remained as a recollection of the past.

The Bisley Camp branch line to the west of Brookwood opened in 1890 and closed in 1952. The object of the short line, about 1¼ miles long, was to link the Bisley Camp of the National Rifle Association (NRA) to the main Waterloo–West of England main line. During the First World War however, the branch was extended westwards to connect the military camps formed at Pirbright, Deepcut and Blackdown.

The original site for the NRA ranges was at Wimbledon Common. In 1864 a tramway was built to convey competitors and spectators from a camp on the common to the ranges. It was a straightforward layout with no points or sidings and the track gauge was 2 ft. Six four-wheeled wagons were provided for passengers which were drawn by military horses running alongside the track rather than between the rails. As can be expected, the tramway proved quite an attraction and it is understood the fares were 2d return and 1d single. In 1877 a steam tramcar was made available to the NRA comprising a boxed-in design and

A funeral train passes Wimbledon on June 25 1902. The train had two 'religious' portions, each with its own hearse van. (Lens of Sutton)

weighing about 4 tons. The locomotive, capable of pulling six fully-loaded wagons, was inaugurated by the Prince of Wales. It was named 'Wharncliffe' and was to play a role in later years at Bisley.

The remains of Bisley Camp branch line at Brookwood station. The track has since been removed. (Lens of Sutton)

When the NRA was given notice to leave Wimbledon Common in 1888, a new site at Bisley was adopted on an area of government land. Two years later, by July 12th 1890, the short branch line from Brookwood to Bisley Camp had been completed. The first train, hauled by an LSWR Adams 02 class 0-4-4 No. 185, conveyed the Prince and Princess of Wales along the line with the engine especially named 'Alexandra' (after the Princess of Wales) for the Royal occasion. At Bisley huge crowds welcomed the Royal guests and the new Bisley line was declared officially open.

When moving from Wimbledon, the NRA had transferred the small tramway to Bisley. By 1898 this had been duly installed to carry competitors and spectators from Bisley Camp station the mile journey to the ranges. Also transferred was the tram engine 'Wharncliffe' and its set of wagons. Soon afterwards a further 2 ft gauge tramway was added to transport targets to the range butts. Although some tracks were later removed, the line to the 'Century' butts survived to be worked currently by a Lister 2-cylinder diesel engine.

When the First World War broke out, the NRA placed its facilities at the disposal of the War Office. Soon Bisley Camp was occupied by regular soldiers and during the first four months of the war, some 150,000 men had undergone training at the site. By 1916 the camps in the area had become quite extensive and it was agreed that an extension from Bisley should be built to include Pirbright, Deepcut and Blackdown to be served by a line about 3 miles long. This was completed by March 1917, with an opening ceremony performed by King George V and Queen Mary whilst visiting soldiers in the area. In 1919 after the war,

Push-and-pull set No. 721 with class M7 0-4-4T No. 1328 at Bisley Camp station c1947. (Lens of Sutton)

the NRA resumed its normal meetings and the 3 mile extension was probably lifted during the early 1920s.

In 1939 at the outset of the Second World War, Bisley again assumed importance as a centre for small arms training and research. Two years later the branch was extended once again but this time only for about one mile to reach the outskirts of Pirbright Camp. After the war, however, the branch and extension were not to survive many years. The Pirbright extension was probably lifted by 1950 and the Brookwood to Bisley Camp closed in early 1952 after over 60 years of faithful service. To mark the closure, the Railway Correspondence and Travel society organised a special journey in November of the same year

Bisley Camp station, July 1987. Much of the line's track had been lifted by 1953 although Bisley Camp platform buildings remained to become home of the Lloyds Bank Rifle Club. The Mk 1 BR Sleeper Car on a short stretch of track provides extra sleeping accommodation for members. (Author)

using a LSWR push-pull set of two coaches borrowed from the *'Wharncliffe', the* Clapham Junction to Kensington service (previously used on the *Merryweather tram engine* Plymouth–Turnchapel service) and hauled by M7 class 0-4-4T *at Bisley Camp c1907.* No. 30027. *(Lens of Sutton)*

The majority of the track was lifted by November 1953, although a spur remained as a siding for many years. Later this was removed and today at Brookwood station only the remains of the Bisley Camp branch bay can be seen. At Bisley Camp station the platform still remains and in 1984 the building became the home of the Lloyds Bank Rifle Club. As a reminder of its railway days, the Lloyds club obtained in 1984, a former Mk 1 BR Sleeping Car which was erected on a short stretch of specially laid track to provide extra sleeping accommodation for club members.

Other reminders of the past can easily be found with platform edges and bridge abutments in evidence. Deepcut Camp station, which survived many years as a Royal Army Ordnance Corps (RAOC) Museum, had a concrete-faced platform but the building was wooden. The walls were made from logs by Canadian troops when the line was first opened in 1917. But even this has now gone since the Museum acquired a new home in 1970 and eventually the station building was demolished. The foundations of an old engine shed and a partly filled-in inspection pit are all that remain of this once fine station.

Chapter 9

BATTLES ALONG
THE CATERHAM VALLEY

Mention 'Halliloo Platform' to any commuters on the comparatively busy Caterham Valley branch line today and they will probably never have heard of it! It was a little-frequented halt consisting of just one platform used from 1897 to 1900 during a period of reconstruction and improvement. Attended mostly by parties of school-children, it was removed when Whyteleafe station opened on January 1st 1900.

When the London & Brighton Railway opened its main line in 1841, the nearest stations to Caterham were at Godstone Road (now Purley) and at Stoats Nest (near Coulsdon). A year later the SER opened a line from Redhill to Tonbridge giving a station at Godstone. Within a few years there was local interest for a line to reach Caterham, although with the village having a population of less than 500 in 1851, the plans were more to reach the local quarries with their fine output of good quality firestone. At that time there was much demand for furnaces, chimneys and hearths and good potential lay beneath the chalk of the North Downs.

The Caterham Railway Company was incorporated although its ideas for lines or possibly tramways to reach quarries near Godstone Hill and War Coppice were not agreed. An Act finally received Royal Approval on June 16th 1854 agreeing the branch as it is known today. The company was an independent one but its activities immediately interested the LBSCR and the SER who were soon to become bitterly involved in battles over the line.

In his book *The Caterham Railway* (Oakwood Press) Jeoffry Spence writes that the single-line track was declared ready for traffic on September 21st 1855 but both the LBSCR and the SER were unwilling to allow the other to work or lease the line, so a series of delays postponed the opening. Finally the Caterham company managed to persuade the LBSCR to let them have 'an engine and two or three carriages' to make an opening of the line possible. The service was inaugurated on August 4th 1856 and public traffic began the next day.

There were two intermediate stations at Kenley (named Coulsdon until December 1856) and Whyteleafe South (Warlingham until 1956). Whyteleafe opened later on January 1st 1900. Godstone Road station (now Purley) was described as 'a single platform with a rough shed for passengers'. The original LBSCR station at the site had closed on September 30th 1847 having been partly dismantled with the platform shelter going to Bexhill station in Sussex.

The LBSCR had refused to re-open its station for, it was

claimed, 'reasons of public safety'. They considered the Caterham Railway to be SER sponsored but when services from Caterham commenced the LBSCR grudgingly gave way. Even then it had not been until a few days beforehand that the Brighton company had agreed to stop their trains to give connections to London and the coast. At this stage, the name of Godstone Road station was changed to Caterham Junction although for a time the Caterham Railway continued to use the old name. Initially there were four trains each way daily with three on Sundays.

At about the same time another proposal came to light. Plans were deposited by 'The South Kent Railway & The Mid Kent Railway' for a widening of the existing Brighton company's line from East Croydon to Caterham Junction plus a rival line to Caterham. The route was planned to reach Godstone and the quarries as originally intended by the Caterham Railway Company. However the whole situation was fraught with problems and the idea never materialised.

From the start the Caterham line did not pay. The railway company tried hard to find passengers by offering season tickets to London at £7 a year first class and £5 a year second class to people building houses on the company's property. Further trouble between the LBSCR and the SER ensued. Because of the earlier delaying tactics, the Caterham company sued the LBSCR. In retaliation, the Brighton company caused trouble over the hire of rolling stock. Meanwhile the LBSCR had been doing its best to acquire the Caterham line by offering less than half its original cost, a move which seriously antagonised the SER. The last hope that the Caterham company might survive was lost when a contractor claimed he was still owed a considerable sum of money and, if not paid, he would pull up the rails. In

Purley station probably in the 1920s. Caterham and Tattenham Corner trains used (as today) the platforms on the right. (Lens of Sutton)

November 1858 the Caterham Railway Company applied for powers to sell or lease the line to the SER.

In 1859, relations improved. The LBSCR had been pressing for a spur, less than half a mile long, leading from Norwood Junction to the Farnborough Extension of the West End of London & Crystal Palace Railway (later owned by the LCDR). On July 7th of that year, the LBSCR got its link and in return the SER obtained full rights to use the Brighton company's Caterham Junction station. It could be considered a poor transaction since the spur was hardly used and then mostly by LCDR trains. It was rarely used after the First World War and was finally closed in 1966. On July 21st 1859, the SER finally

acquired the Caterham Railway for £15,200 – it cost almost £40,000!

However, the battle between the giants was by no means over. Following disputes elsewhere over territory, relations worsened and in 1862 the LBSCR forbade the use of East Croydon station to the SER insisting that all passengers arriving from the Caterham branch should hold LBSCR tickets. In further aggravation, the LBSCR then timed trains to leave Caterham Junction before branch passengers could possibly rebook. Worse was still to come when passengers were forcibly prevented from boarding SER trains at Caterham Junction. Finally it was the floods of complaints published in *The Times*, then at the height of its power, which compelled the Brighton company to give way.

Bad feelings rankled on for many years. With the Caterham branch still firmly in SER hands, plans were deposited in 1873 by a company called the South Caterham Railway for another line to run from Purley (still known as Caterham Junction) via Old Coulsdon to Upper Caterham. The idea for a second railway, like the previous one in 1856, was not practicable and it also failed.

Two years later in 1875 an interesting scheme was put forward by the Metropolitan & Brighton Railway. Proceeding southwards from Beckenham, tracks would have passed closed to Warlingham village to cross the Woldingham Valley Road by viaduct. After negotiating a tunnel under Tillingdown trains would have reached Caterham close to the present station. Further south trains would cross to East Grinstead before travelling via Lindfield to Brighton. The idea of course came to nothing and Caterham did not get its direct link with the coast.

On October 1st 1888 Caterham Junction was renamed Purley. According to records it acquired its name from the Pirelea family

Kenley station, August 1987. The road and the traffic have changed but the building remains much the same. (Author)

WHYTELEAFE STATION

who once owned the district with one ancestor, Reginald de Pirle, dating back to 1332. The change had followed pressure from the Post Office who were complaining that mail for Caterham Junction was finishing up in Caterham.

At the end of 1899 work began to double the track and improve the service. This was completed by January 1st 1900, by which time Caterham station had been rebuilt and the old station demolished. A new station opened at Whyteleafe. In August 1900, the SER and LCDR obtained powers to build from the Croydon-Oxted line (opened in 1884) near Sanderstead to link with both the Caterham and Tattenham Corner lines avoiding Purley completely. Apart from joining two SER routes and the joint SER/LBSCR (Oxted) line, this could have served as a useful connection in the years to come in an area of complex commuter lines but it was never built.

Inevitably competition was to come from motorbuses. In the booklet *Caterham and Warlingham – Jubilee History* (The Bourne Society), Jeoffry Spence tells an amusing account as to how in 1907 Caterham got its first (unofficial) vehicles. Apparently buses used earlier in Hastings had failed because of competition from electric trams. After the fleet had been laid up over the winter of 1906–7, trouble was anticipated because of certain unpaid accounts so in April 1907 all the buses set out for London. Many of them failed to travel more than a few miles but two, still able to climb hills, got away. One eventually reached Tonbridge before giving up the ghost and the other expired at the top of River Hill, Sevenoaks. Both were brought on to Caterham where one was repaired with parts from the other. The two drivers then ran this bus providing a service between Caterham and Godstone cover-

ing a route where twice previously trains had failed to establish themselves. Eventually the bus was withdrawn since it was not adequately licensed and a regular service did not commence until 1914.

Whyteleafe station, August 1987. The station opened when the track doubling was completed in 1900. (Author)

All was continuing peacefully on the Caterham Valley line with the stations building up useful commuter traffic. On March 25th 1928 'third rail' electric trains reached Tattenham Corner and Caterham, some of the earliest to be used in the Central section.

Caterham station which opened on August 5, 1856 after bitter squabbles between rival railway companies. Seen here c1910. (Lens of Sutton)

It was not until January 1933 that electric services reached Brighton, Hove and Worthing. Services improved on the Caterham line and building development was evident everywhere along the valley.

There are only a few reminders of the old days along the line – perhaps the best example is the attractive high gabled station house at Kenley. More typical of today is the CCTV double barrier crossing at Whyteleafe station. Yet part of the old ancestry is still evident. For many years now weekday trains (peak times excepted) for Caterham and Tattenham Corner have left half-hourly from Charing Cross reflecting the times when Charing Cross was an SER station.

Chapter 10

FROM EPSOM TO HORSHAM
VIA BOX HILL

Epsom's first railway station was situated near the east end of the High Street. Earlier it had been expected that atmospheric trains from the London & Croydon railway (to become part of the LBSCR from 1846) would reach the town but, due to their lack of success (Chapter 3), it was finally steam trains that arrived from West Croydon on May 10th 1847. Earlier in 1845 a line had been proposed by an independent company, the South Western & Epsom Junction Railway, to reach Epsom from Wimbledon and then to be sold or leased to the LSWR. The idea came to nothing, although a similar line was to follow later.

The LBSCR had completed its coastal route from London to Portsmouth via Brighton in 1847. When the LSWR's Portsmouth Direct line opened in 1859, the LBSCR was obliged to shorten its own to remain competitive and at the same time keep the LSWR out of West Sussex. Thus a cut-off route via Horsham to be known as the Mid-Sussex line and saving over eight miles came to be considered.

The Epsom & Leatherhead Railway company had been formed in 1856 but when the line opened on February 1st 1859, it had become a joint LBSCR/LSWR venture, largely to overcome a threat by the latter to build a line from Wimbledon to Dorking. By April 4th 1859, the LSWR had completed a line from Wimbledon to Epsom and because of this Epsom had now acquired two railway stations – the new LSWR station on the present site and the LBSCR Epsom (later Epsom Town) station

The LBSCR station at Epsom (later Epsom Town) which was closed to passengers in 1929. (Lens of Sutton)

An ex-LCDR Class R 0-4-4T in SR livery at Boxhill & Westhumble station in the late 1920s when the station was known as 'Boxhill & Burford Bridge'. (Lens of Sutton)

near the High Street (closed to passengers in 1929).

The first service to Leatherhead was provided by the LSWR on February 1st 1859, with Brighton company trains following on August 8th of the same year when a link between the two Epsom stations had been built. Initially the line was single and an LSWR timetable of 1860 recommended to intending passengers that 'an extra five minutes should be taken on each journey' whilst the line was newly-built! Rivalry between the companies remained. When the LSWR had built its station at the junction of the lines at Epsom, the track layout had been designed in such a way that LBSCR trains were located on through centre tracks and thus prevented from calling at the platforms.

Throughout its railway days, Leatherhead could boast three railway stations. The first was the jointly owned LSWR/LBSCR terminus which was situated just north of the Kingston Road. This lasted just eight years, to be closed when the LBSCR extended to Dorking, opening its own station to the south at today's site and the LSWR building a separate station close by.

The Leatherhead to Dorking line began services on March 11th 1867 at about the same time the line from Epsom to Leatherhead was doubled, giving double track throughout. By 1st May the same year, trains had reached Horsham connecting with the existing 1848 line from Three Bridges and also the route from Horsham to the coast which had been completed four years earlier. In 1885 the LSWR reached Effingham Junction from its Leatherhead station to connect with the New Guildford line from Hampton Court Junction to Guildford which had opened in the same year.

The situation with rival stations virtually side by side at Leatherhead lasted until 1927 when post-Grouping rationalisation took over. The Southern Railway altered the layout by providing a new bridge over Station Road for the Effingham Junction line with the result that the former LSWR station could

be closed.

Today only the old LBSCR station remains with its fine herring-bone brickwork pattern and ornamental tower. On the down side the numerous arches cannot fail to impress and the decaying chimney was recently restored with matching bricks. The station building is now a listed structure. For many years the old LSWR track remained parallel to the 'new' through track for use as carriage sidings but today even this has been lifted and the area built over. Nothing is left of the original 1859 station except an old engine shed that continued in use until 1874. Afterwards the shed was leased out as a church and school at £15 a year and in 1986 it had survived as an engineering works.

Journeying southwards through the 530 yard long Mickleham Tunnel and crossing the river Mole, the station of Boxhill and Westhumble is reached. Popular with walkers throughout the years, the station, opened with the line in 1867, was attractively built to match its surroundings thanks to the stipulations of the original landowner. The main complex is on the down side with the station building steeply gabled in the French style and with decorative tiles and an ornate tower. Originally opened as West Humble, the station has had many name changes acquiring its present title after four variations!

Not far from the station, just off the A24, visiting travellers can find a public house called the *Stepping Stones*. This is named after the well-known stones of the same name which cross the nearby river Mole providing the start of one of the routes to Box Hill's summit. The sight from the top will not disappoint those who struggle up its steep paths. On a clear day there is a splendid bird's eye view of Dorking and the many villages beyond. The viewpoint itself is a large memorial recalling the memory of Sir Leopold Salomons of Norbury Park who first gave land in the area to the National Trust.

Not far away some 90 yards west from the old fort building,

there is a stone with a strange inscription. For this spot once marked the grave of Major Peter Labelliere, a Marines Officer, who was an eccentric of Dorking. Having correctly forecast the date of his death in 1800, he asked to be buried upside down on Box Hill. Since he had considered the world had 'turned topsy-turvey', he reckoned he would therefore be right at the end! Today he is remembered by his stone but it is said his body was later removed and buried elsewhere.

It is considered that Box Hill acquired its name (it was previously called White Hill) when box trees were planted there during the reign of Charles I by the Earl of Arundel. Apparently the trees grew abundantly with stems of nearly 9 inches in diameter and the wood was highly prized for its close fine grain and its beautiful golden colour with products including chessmen, parts of musical instruments and decorative inlay for fine furniture. By the early 19th century the box trees had gone and only bushes remained.

Continuing southwards, the next station is Dorking North which was opened as 'Dorking'. The name was changed in 1923 to avoid confusion with the SER Dorking station which became Dorking Town. Some of Dorking (North)'s earlier buildings have survived the years on the down island platform but on the up side the station facilities have been tastefully combined in a commercial development. Electrification came to the Epsom–Leatherhead–Dorking North route on July 12th 1925, at the same time as the old LSWR link from Leatherhead to Effingham Junction. It was considered a speculative venture since many of the areas were still rural, but it proved very successful. At Dorking North alone, the sale of season tickets more than quadrupled in only eight years.

Less than two months after trains had arrived at Dorking, a new line opened to Horsham with services commencing on May 1st 1867. At the same time a spur was opened linking the LBSCR line with the SER east-west line although this was little used (see Chapter 6). Intermediate stations were Holmwood, Ockley (for a time known as 'Ockley and Capel') and Warnham (in Sussex). The whole route from Leatherhead to Horsham was in fact promoted by an independent concern, the Horsham, Dorking & Leatherhead company but, in 1864, a year after its approval to proceed, it had been amalgamated with the LBSCR.

Holmwood station, unlike many on the route, was built on a bridge across the track. In its time it has enjoyed quite an extensive goods yard with gunpowder vans often seen in the sidings bringing materials for the nearby Schermuly Pistol Rocket Works where the 'Verey Light' signal flares were made. The goods yard closed in 1964 although the goods shed had been demolished earlier in 1958 since it had become unsafe. Surprisingly a solitary up siding was electrified in 1938 and for many years a London stopping service terminated there every hour using the siding when not required. The siding was lengthened in

1961 to accommodate new rolling stock but fell from use as recently as 1975.

Ockley, like its neighbour also once had numerous sidings. Dating back to the last century, an extensive 11 acre brickyard, Le Steeres of Jayes Park, stood close by and up to three wagons of bricks a week left the area. The works closed in 1914 but bricks were railed out again from 1938 from the nearby Phorpres Works. There was an Army Command Supply Depot at nearby Okewood Hill during the last war which gave additional heavy traffic.

In the book *Southern Main Lines – Epsom to Horsham*, Vic Mitchell and Keith Smith write of a substantial 'memorial bush' on the down side about two miles south of Ockley. According to local hearsay, it was planted and tended in memory of a ganger who was struck by a locomotive whilst walking to the Northwood up distant, for fog signalling duty. At Northwood the signal box was erected in 1899 to meet increasing traffic. It had only four levers in use and was manned only at peak times until it ceased to be used after 1956. Apparently when the machine room window was broken, it was never repaired since this would have disturbed the nesting routine of some local house martins!

As part of the Mid Sussex line, the route from Epsom to Horsham remains a busy one but sadly many intermediate stations seem much neglected with staff manning at peak times only. When the author visited Ockley in February 1987, it appeared deserted. The once fine building still stands and in the wall a letter box, still in use, bears the letters V R giving evidence of its age. One hears that attempts have been made to register Ockley station as a listed building. If efforts remain unsuccessful, must it be that Ockley, like many others on the route, will in time be demolished with such fine structures lost for ever?

The LBSCR Dorking station (North) c1910 looking south. A B2X class 4-4-0 awaits departure and a Stroudley D1 0-4-2T stands in the bay. Note the typical LBSCR round-ended wagons on the right. (Lens of Sutton)

Chapter 11

A DAY AT CROYDON RACES –
ADDISCOMBE AND WOODSIDE

Trains first reached Beckenham (now Beckenham Junction) station from New Cross in 1857 along a branch line constructed by the Mid-Kent & North Kent Junction Railway. When opened it was leased to the SER and it was not until 1864 that trains reached Croydon (Addiscombe Road) – now known as Addiscombe – leaving the original Beckenham branch at New Beckenham, a station which was opened with the Addiscombe line.

New Beckingham station lasted only three months and the present station on a new site was built in 1866/7. Leaving New Beckenham today the now little-used curve to Beckenham Junction can still be seen – singled as recently as the early 1980s. The original New Beckenham station can be located just before passing under the Victoria – Orpington line. Initially Elmers End was the only intermediate station on the Addiscombe line with Woodside opening in 1871 and Clock House in 1890. In 1880 the West Wickham & Hayes Company was incorporated but this was acquired by the SER in 1881. Trains reached Hayes from Elmers End in 1882.

Meantime in 1878 the LBSCR and SER had reached an agreement on the construction of a line from Croydon to Oxted (and beyond) and Section 18 of the Act specified that the two companies were to share ownership. With their line now reaching Addiscombe, it was to be expected that the SER would want access to the new (shared) Oxted line. This would also provide it with an alternative route from London via the Mid-Kent line

The wooden signalbox with its semaphore signalling at Addiscombe station, March 1986. Beyond are the carriage sheds said to be haunted! (Author)

thus avoiding the LBSCR stations of New Cross (later New Cross Gate), East and South Croydon.

Such a line received authority in August 1880, when approval was given to the independent Woodside and South Croydon company to go ahead. It was planned to build a route leaving the Addiscombe branch at a point immediately south of Woodside station to link with the Oxted line south of South Croydon just after the latter had left the main Brighton line. In 1882 the independent company was acquired by the LBSCR and SER jointly.

Considerable earthworks and numerous bridges were necessary to complete the line. Three short tunnels were built quite close together to be known as Woodside, Park Hill and Coombe Lane.

Woodside station which opened in 1871 to serve a nearby racecourse. (Lens of Sutton)

An ex-SER 118 class No. 4A 2-4-0 (built in 1860) at Coombe Road with an unusual assortment of stock c1902. (Lens of Sutton)

An SECR railcar approaches Coombe Road (opened as Coombe Lane in 1885) c1906. (Lens of Sutton)

In all some eight over or under bridges were necessary and it was not until August 10th 1885 that services could begin. At the fork where the Oxted line was joined, a station was built called Selsdon Road (later Selsdon and now closed). Initially the only intermediate station was Coombe Lane (later Coombe Road) but two stations were to follow in 1906 being Bingham Road and Spencer Road Halt.

During the First World War, the intermediate stations closed. In March 1915, Bingham Road and Spencer Road Halt closed and in January 1917, Coombe Road followed suit. Spencer Road Halt, located off Croham Road not far from the present South Croydon station, never re-opened but Bingham Road and Coombe Road came into use again in September 1935, when the line was electrified. Even so, Bingham Road was relegated to becoming a halt. Electric services ran stopping trains between Charing Cross and Sanderstead using the Woodside–Selsdon line and became known as the 'Sanderstead Electrics'. It was never heavily used except for local commuting. The author has fond school-day memories of travelling the long-winded route from Charing Cross right through to Sanderstead – often in an empty compartment – just for the sheer enjoyment of rail travel!

The Addiscombe line was electrified earlier in 1926 at the same time as the branch to Hayes. Addiscombe station still retains its 19th century building and trains use two faces of a single platform. At the London end of the platform there is a wooden signal box controlling the local workings which, at the time of the author's visit (1985) included semaphore signalling. Now more widely used than the station are the carriage sidings and a four bay shed on the down side used to store and clean EMU stock.

According to writer W.B. Herbert in his book *Railway Ghosts*, the carriage sheds are haunted! Apparently at night, when stock is berthed, the vehicles are isolated from the third rail and the hand brakes screwed down tightly for safety reasons. But on more than one occasion, the brake compressors have been heard running even though disconnected. Each time the shunter has to again 'cut out' the train. In addition carriage doors are heard to open and close and, perhaps strangest of all, trains are heard to move in the shed.

It seems that many years ago a shunter was killed between two units while coupling a train and some think he 'returns' to carry out these frequent manifestations. On one occasion a shunter witnessed an apparition when waiting outside the sheds. He saw a figure in grey coming out of the building walking towards him and was very frightened. But the features were blurred and then suddenly the figure disappeared. The truth of these stories is of course doubted by some but, it still has to be said, there certainly have been many strange happenings here over the past years.

Perhaps Woodside was once one of the more important stations since, apart from being a minor junction, it also at one time served the nearby Croydon Race-course. Horses were often brought to the race-course by train and, for a number of years, a track to the course from the down side of the station catered for many of the famous horses of the time. To this day, a doorway with a high arch exists close to the ticket barrier, constructed so that horses could reach the adjacent Ashburton Park without climbing to the road level.

The race-course had been established at Stroud Green around 1862 and was located opposite Ashburton Park, now the site of Ashburton High School. A number of race meetings were held each year with an important steeple-chase event in March from which many fine horses were engaged for the United Kingdom Grand Handicap. This Croydon meeting occupied a high position in the steeple-chasing world, equivalent to that of Epsom in flat racing. Aintree was still a lesser rival.

The race-course at Woodside was important enough to attract many well known people of the time including the Duke of Hamilton, Lord Beresford and Mr Richard Marsh (the Royal trainer). It was such popularity that had induced the railway company to open the station at Woodside in 1871. By 1885 with a link to the Oxted line completed, more people were coming to the races. Two years later in 1887 came Queen Victoria's Golden Jubilee and to mark the occasion 10,500 school children joined in celebrations held on the race-course. The area was at the height of its popularity.

However, the railway which had encouraged the number of visitors was now becoming its downfall. Crowds increased and there was insufficient supervision. It was claimed that too many undesirable people were coming to the area and efforts were getting under way to bring about closure of the track. By the end of 1890, the local movement for the abolition of Croydon Races was successful and the local licensing authority refused to grant a regular renewal. The last meetings took place on November 25th and 26th 1890, and a quiet locality many miles to the south called Gatwick was inaugurated as a successor.

Until the Second World War the area became the home of Beckenham Golf Club. Subsequently it was a site for the Woodside Fire Station and the stables in Lower Addiscombe Road were used as winter quarters for a circus. The stables gave way to a housing estate and where the entrance to the saddling paddock and grandstand from Shirley Road once stood, Shirley Park Road can now be found.

As for the railways, the Addiscombe branch line still remains but the Woodside to Selsdon line closed in May 1983. Except for a freight siding at Selsdon, most of the track had been broken up by March 1985. Woodside station is still there of course but the race-course is very much a thing of the past having closed almost one hundred years ago. It is doubtful if many of the local residents of today even know it had existed.

Chapter 12

TRAINS TO EPSOM RACECOURSE

First ideas to reach Epsom Racecourse by rail came in 1838 when the railway authorities arranged for trains on the newly opened London & Southampton Railway to be stopped near the present Surbiton station – then called Kingston. Eight trains were planned on race-days and passengers were set down at a point where the Kingston to Epsom Road crossed the line, to finish the six mile journey on foot or by cart or trap.

The service began on Derby Day but many were disappointed. Over 5,000 people besieged the then London terminus at Nine Elms and, although several trains got away, the crowd eventually invaded the station and the police had to be called to restore order. Another route came four years later, also well patronised, when the London & Brighton Railway made similar arrangements for trains to take race-goers to Stoat's Nest (between Coulsdon and Purley) after which a walk or ride of over seven miles was necessary.

Race-going on Epsom Downs has long had its place in history. Pepys' diary of 1660 tells of 'horse racing that took place daily at noon, and cudgel-playing, wrestling, hawking and foot racing in the afternoon'. First records of horse races go back to about the time of James I's residence at Nonsuch around 1610. With the opening of the Wells later in the century following the 'discovery'

An LBSCR Stroudley D1 0-4-2T approaches Sutton from Epsom Downs in 1883. (Lens of Sutton)

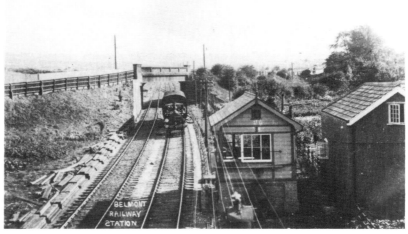

of the world famous Epsom Salts, the Downs became even more popular with greatly increased numbers coming to the area.

It was not until 1844 that a railway to reach Epsom was first considered. An independent company, the South Western & Epsom Junction Railway, planned a line with the prospect of selling or letting it to the LSWR. The idea came to nothing although a similar scheme was to come later.

By 1847 the LBSCR – previously the London & Brighton Railway – had reached Epsom from West Croydon and 12 years later in 1859 the LSWR had reached Epsom from Raynes Park. Race traffic continued to increase and it was clear a station was needed much nearer to the course itself. There was much rivalry

Banstead Station.

between the companies but it was the LBSCR who eventually won the day when it took over a concern called the Banstead & Epsom Downs Railway Company which had been formed to build such a branch leaving the existing line in Sutton.

During construction, an attempt had been made to build the terminus only 200 yards or so from the Grandstand. Such efforts were frustrated by strong opposition from the Epsom Grandstand Association which was supported by John Briscoe M.P., Lord of the Manor and Freeholder of Epsom Downs. Eventually the problem was resolved by John Briscoe who sold the plot on which the present Epsom Downs station stands, over half a mile away from the course. It was not until 1901, some 36 years later, that the South Eastern Railway opened a station at Tattenham Corner much closer to the course (see chapter 16).

First trains from Sutton to Epsom Downs ran on May 22nd 1865 – just in time for the Derby. Results exceeded expectations and, on Derby Day alone, some 70,000 people travelled by the new railway. The line was double track from the beginning to accommodate the traffic expected. The vast terminus boasted nine platforms with 'middle sidings' to house additional trains or to be used for 'engine release'. The platforms were not covered and the only roofed area was part of the terminal building behind the buffer stops. There was a 42 ft turntable and a tank house with water columns which were placed at the end of four platforms and a siding.

The station-master at Epsom Downs must have been a busy man at times for, in addition to his normal duties, he also ran a nearby amusement park – with company approval of course. On occasions other than race-days, the only traffic of note was the

Banstead station 1984. The station building has changed little since last century. (Author)

73

comings and goings of students to a nearby college and also numerous school parties or Sunday school outings. For the latter two, station signs even included 'Boys' and 'Girls'!

At about this time an unexpected threat to the new branch came from the rival LCDR which was planning a line between Herne Hill and Epsom. However, when the LBSCR offered attractive through bookings, without change of train for the race traffic as well as intermediate stations, the scheme was withdrawn.

Prior to the new line, Sutton had been a small two-platform station affair but, when the Epsom Downs branch began, new waiting rooms and booking offices were built. These were situated mainly in the fork of the old lines and the new tracks, the latter curving away sharply to the south from the double-track junction to the east of the station. The first station to be reached was called California, known today as Belmont.

How it acquired its original name relates to a local resident charged with poaching. At the time the punishment was transportation but the victim did not fancy this idea so he escaped to America to eventually join the California gold rush from which he became quite rich. When he returned to this country he built a public house and called it the *California Arms* and it was from this that the local station took its name.

Troubles soon followed since goods destined for the area were frequently exported to California, U.S.A.! So, the poor station-master, burdened with complaints for lost consignments and fearing for his health, asked that the station should be renamed Belmont. The LBSCR agreed and it was changed in 1875.

The *California Arms* became *The California* but recently this too changed its name and is now known as *Belmonts*. The present building was erected in 1955 since, during the last war, the pub suffered serious bomb damage in April 1941 when 10 people were killed and many injured. It was here that Private Gibb distinguished himself when, for three hours, he held up loose debris while buried women were rescued. For his outstanding efforts he was awarded the BEM and a plaque on the present public house wall commemorates the event.

At California station there was initially a goods yard between a level crossing and the Brighton Road bridge. The area was very restricted and a wagon turntable was necessary but, when the level crossing was replaced in 1888 by the present steeply humped bridge, the sidings were moved to the east of the Brighton Road. Before entering Banstead station, the line enters a steep cutting in the downs. The chalk excavated was dumped on either side of the track and this has now of course become overgrown. Yet these 'lumps' can still be remembered by some as 'the chalk hills'.

By 1891 local interests at the upper end of the Chipstead Valley decided it would be to their advantage if a railway were

built to serve their area. The group, headed by Mr Cosmo Bonsor, a Director of the Bank of England, considered the best route would be from the Banstead area on the Epsom Downs line to reach Tadworth through a long tunnel. In 1892 the idea gained Parliamentary approval under the title of the Epsom Downs Extension Railway Act. But difficulties arose and finance was not forthcoming – also the LBSCR was not interested in supporting such a scheme. When plans were later submitted to consider a railway along the Chipstead Valley (Chapter 16), the Epsom Downs Extension Railway idea was revived for a time to give a possible link between Purley, Epsom Downs and Sutton. Support for the scheme appeared to continue but when renewed powers, agreed in 1897 for two years, lapsed, the idea was forgotten.

Two Brighton-built Fairburn 2-6-4 tank locomotives head a race-special at Epsom Downs station in the early 1950s. (Lens of Sutton)

In 1898 Banstead station was renamed Banstead and Burgh Heath, only to be called Banstead again in August 1928. Also in 1928 DC third rail electrification was completed to Epsom Downs to include six platforms at the terminus. At the same time the down platforms at Belmont and Banstead were extended to take 8-car trains. From an annual number of passengers using the branch in 1927 at just under 330,000, the number rose by 1935 to more than 850,000. When the locomotive turntable at Epsom Downs was removed, electric trains were more than assured of popularity.

Decline of the branch, as with many, began some 30 years ago. Cars were taking the place of trains and services were cut. From June 1961 there was a cut-back on early and late services and just over a year later most off-peak trains from London Bridge terminated at Sutton. The introduction of the 5-day week in the

late 1950s for most commuters killed off much of the Saturday traffic. In 1972 five platforms were abandoned at Epsom Downs and nine years later single line working was introduced using the up-line. Users of the line today must indeed be anxious about the branch's future.

Gone are the thousands of race-goers of the past who arrived often in Pullman Car 'Race Specials'. Gone too are the Derby days when trains thundered through a crowded Sutton station, often double-headed, to tackle the 1 in 60 gradient up to Banstead. Surely watching the races on TV today cannot give quite the same excitement!

Chapter 13

THE HORSHAM AND GUILDFORD
DIRECT RAILWAY

It was well over 40 years ago when Christmas shoppers and commuters alike were shot up and bombed by German aircraft on the Horsham to Guildford branch line near Bramley and Wonersh station. The plane, a Dornier 217, first machine-gunned the Guildford-bound train and then released a bomb which exploded in the railway bank as the train was passing. The date was December 16th 1942.

Speaking to the author in October 1987, Mrs Ruth Bailey of Godalming vividly remembered the incident. On the day in question she sat with her back to the front of the train which comprised just two carriages pushed by a small 'Puffing Billy'. She recalled, 'The plane attacked from the front and I heard the bullets hit, saw the plane as it flew over very low and felt the bomb explode almost instantaneously. The train halted just as it approached the first gardens in Bramley.' Her impression was that help arrived incredibly quickly, including a number of Canadian soldiers one of whom took her to hospital in a jeep.

Battles along the line began much earlier dating back to 1860 when the Horsham & Guildford Direct Railway Company was first incorporated. There had been a strong body of opinion favouring a route south from Cranleigh through Alfold to join the Pulborough line, 1½ miles south of Adversane. The Horsham route of course prevailed but already there was division between the LSWR and the LBSCR both wanting to take over ownership of the independent company. Further problems developed over

Bramley station opened in October 1865 and became Bramley and Wonersh in June 1888. The line lasted almost 100 years. (Lens of Sutton)

construction and at one stage the contractor went bankrupt causing a £30,000 loss. Finally in 1864 the LBSCR succeeded in taking over the line even though at that stage it was incomplete.

As soon as the line opened on October 2nd 1865, there was trouble at Rudgwick station. Following an inspection of the track, it had been decreed that trains could not stop there since the gradient on which it was built was too steep at 1 in 80. It was another month before the station was opened and then only after it was completely rebuilt and a new bridge constructed over the river Arun.

Trouble was soon to erupt again. At the southern end, the line joined the Horsham to Pulborough 'Mid Sussex' route at Christ's Hospital station before turning north east to Horsham. At Christ's Hospital, a spur had been built to link Guildford with a junction at Itchingfield to give access to the Pulborough and Steyning lines so that through trains were possible from the Midlands to the South Coast. However the LBSCR closed this fork within two years since it was afraid its rival, the LSWR, would gain access to Sussex by using this section. Today there are no remains of this spur and the ground has been ploughed up.

Initially the service on the new line was good. There were eight trains daily with evening trains from Guildford to Cranleigh. Another service provided late trains from Horsham to Cranleigh twice weekly. However the local press were less optimistic about its future. The *West Sussex Gazette* of October 10th 1865, commented, the line was 'likely to prove a more picturesque than profitable part of the system of the London–Brighton Railway Company'.

Before 1867 Cranleigh was spelt 'Cranley'. The change to the present spelling was made at the request of the Post Office to avoid confusion with Crawley in Sussex on badly-written envelopes and parcels. Cranleigh as a village has numerous claims to fame. Opposite the parish church of St. Nicholas, the hospital, founded in 1859 by local surgeon Mr A. Napper, was the first 'cottage hospital' of its kind in the country. Today it has considerably extended but the original 16th century house is still there. The church too is interesting. The pillar bases have a 'claw' decoration and the carved head below the south transept is that of a cat. Local residents believe it gave Lewis Carroll the inspiration for his Cheshire Cat in 'Alice in Wonderland'.

Unfortunately traffic on the Cranleigh line (as it became known) was not as good as expected and fares rose only 18 months after the opening. Even so the line continued quietly through the years with some useful passenger and freight traffic. Much of the commuter traffic came from Cranleigh and there was freight from private sidings, especially at Baynards. In later years the platform at Baynards became renowned for its fine display of dahlias but unfortunately there were few passengers there to see it.

In 1896 the Light Railway Act was passed which meant that many Board of Trade requirements could be waived under certain circumstances. Under this Act, plans were deposited in the same year for a light railway to run from Ockley, on the Dorking–Horsham line, to Selham, on the Pulborough-Midhurst line, with connections to be made at Cranleigh. Nothing transpired but in 1898–9 another scheme was launched for a 'normal' railway to connect Cranleigh with Holmwood, south of Dorking. Again nothing happened but had either of these transpired, then Cranleigh could have indeed become quite a sizeable and important junction.

During the First World War, the line proved its usefulness as a through route by transporting soldiers and equipment from the Midlands via Guildford and Horsham to the ports of Newhaven and Littlehampton. Otherwise little changed with services continuing normally until 1917 when Sunday services were withdrawn as a wartime economy measure.

There was quite an occasion for Cranleigh School in 1935 when the 'Schools', class 4-4-0 express locomotive of the same

A passenger train near Bramley station after having been shot up and bombed by a German aircraft in December 1942. Fortunately a side corridor ran half the length of the coach otherwise injuries would have been worse. Seven people were killed in the incident and many injured. (Middleton Press)

A BR (ex-LBSCR) Class D3 0-4-4T No. 32379 push-pull at Baynards, January 1950. (Lens of Sutton)

name visited the village to be placed on exhibition at the station. This class of locomotives had been introduced in the 1930s. Cranleigh School had been founded for the education of farmers' sons and was recognised as a public school in 1898.

At one stage in the late 1930s there was talk of electrifying the line from Guildford to Cranleigh, providing a continuation of the Waterloo via Cobham service. Existing electric services to Guildford had a 30 minute wait before returning to Waterloo and the idea seemed feasible but nothing happened and when the Second World War came, any ideas were completely shelved.

Following the outbreak of war, the line once again assumed an important role. Its usefulness as a through route was proved with the movement of troops and munitions. Baynards became a centre for military supplies and special trains used the station because a munitions dump had been set up in the park. There were frequent air attacks along the line but only one serious incident occurred as related at the beginning of this chapter. Nevertheless signal boxes in the area remained open 24 hours a day so that signalmen could report damage to any part of the line during the night.

It was probably the 1955 railway strike that began the decline of the branch. All services ceased during the period and freight traffic suffered badly, never to return to its previous level. The line was now losing money. At the same time the railways were not helping themselves. Trains were leaving Horsham a few minutes before possible connections yet there was a 15 minute wait at Cranleigh. The line had outlived its usefulness and when closure proposals were announced in 1963, they came as no surprise.

An enquiry was held at Cranleigh Village Hall but protests

against the closure were minimal. With such a poor service so little used, there was no hope. The last train left Guildford on June 14th 1965, at 6.55 pm. and returned at 8.34 pm. Boys from Christ's Hospital School sang *Abide with Me* as the train pulled out.

There are numerous recollections of the line today which can be found. Baynards station is now privately owned and has been tastefully restored. The engine shed is still there and the platforms are very much as they were before the station closed in 1965. But for the absence of track, one could be convinced that the railway had not gone. In contrast, Cranleigh has completely disappeared – its site is an open area known as Stockland Square. Goods sidings existed in the area between today's Gateway Foodmarket and the National Westminster Bank and the station

Baynards station, now privately owned, closed in 1965. It has been tastefully restored by its new owners with the platforms, buildings and engine shed appearing much as before. (Author)

A Stroudley D1 tank locomotive with a short train of 4-wheeled stock at Cranleigh, c1900. (Lens of Sutton)

Cranleigh station and goods yard have disappeared today and the area is now known as Stockland Square. The platforms were sited behind the shops where a car park is now available. At the far end there was a level-crossing across Knowle Lane. (Author)

platforms were situated along the car park to the rear of the shops.

Finally Bramley and Wonersh station is now, among other things, a builders yard. Fragments of the platform buildings exist and in one part a postbox marked VR still functions. Although mostly lost in undergrowth, the platform edges remain and when visited in July 1987 the large wooden station nameboard was still there! It was half hidden among the trees proudly reading BRAMLEY AND WONERSH.

Chapter 14

RIVALS SHARE THE OXTED LINE

In the 1865 session of Parliament, a Bill was presented by the independent Surrey & Sussex Junction Railway (S&SJR) for a new line from Croydon to Tunbridge Wells via Oxted to be worked by the LBSCR. This immediately incensed the SER who claimed that it was in breach of a 1864 agreement that neither should violate the other's territory. In an earlier agreement in 1848, the two companies had accepted that any territory north of the Redhill–Tonbridge line and east of the London–Brighton line was available only to the SER. The LBSCR defended its action by stating that the line was merely to shorten its route to Tunbridge Wells (from Croydon via Groombridge) and pointed out that the SER was attempting the same by its planned Sevenoaks 'cut-off' route to Tonbridge.

The S&SJR's Bill was passed on July 6th 1865, and in direct conflict, the SER in 1866, merging unexpectedly with its old rival the London, Chatham & Dover Railway (LCDR), gained Parliamentary approval to build a line from Beckenham to Brighton. To be known as the London, Lewes & Brighton Railway, the route would be through the North Downs near Tatsfield, across to Limpsfield and then southwards to East Grinstead, Sheffield Park and Lewes. Approaching Brighton from the Rottingdean area, a 900 yard tunnel or covered-way was proposed leading to a 'rival' Brighton terminus at the Steine.

BR No. 42013 – apparently not long ex-works – at Riddlesdown station with a set of ex-SR Maunsell coaches. (Lens of Sutton)

Needless to say, neither proposal materialised. 1866 was a bad year for the railways with most suffering severe cash problems. In the same year, a further 'competitive' route proposed by the LBSCR along the Ouse Valley in Sussex, from the Brighton line south of Balcombe across to Sheffield Park and Uckfield, had failed for the same reason but only after some work had been carried out. No work had been done on the SER/LCDR-backed London, Lewes and Brighton line but a good deal of heavy construction had been completed on the S&SJR venture.

North of Oxted, a 2,261 yard tunnel had been bored in addition to two shorter ones along the line. Few bridges had been completed but a brick viaduct north of Woldingham was apparently finished. During construction, there had been many problems. Land deals were found to be 'irregular' and there had been bad rioting at Edenbridge because of large numbers of navvies imported from Belgium. Despite the railway companies' financial problems, the 'territorial dispute' continued and eventually the Duke of Richmond was asked to arbitrate. This resulted in the S&SJR being passed to LBSCR ownership who were immediately anxious to abandon the project. Calculating that it would cost them up to £2 million pounds to complete the line, the company, still short of cash, decided it was easier to pay a £50 per day penalty clause with a maximum limit of £32,250.

SR No. 2477 Class E4X with a mixed selection of coaches at Oxted c1936. (Lens of Sutton)

Nothing positive happened until nearly ten years later by which time much of the S&SJR earthworks had been almost forgotten. During the interim, a further attempt by the LCDR/SER to reach Brighton had been considered, this time via Caterham and East Grinstead, but this plan, like others at the

time, came to nothing. Eventually in 1878, the Croydon, Oxted & East Grinstead Railway (CO&EGR) obtained approval to construct a line. In the same year there was agreement between the rivals LBSCR and SER that they should share the new CO&EGR line from South Croydon to Crowhurst Junction North (where a loop would join with the existing SER Redhill–Tonbridge line). From the loop southwards to East Grinstead it would be totally LBSCR owned.

As soon as work on the line started, there were delays. Under pressure from landowners and prospective users, navvies were imported to speed up the work. But, as had happened thirteen years previously, there was trouble. A local newspaper of May 1882, stated, 'Lingfield Navvies assault Police: Scripture Reader puts in good plea for defence'. Apparently the navvies' disturbing presence in the area had been felt for some time during which time a Chaplain had attended them at their 'Lingfield huts'. A chapel was used at Dormansland and some navvies received baptism. However, despite good influences trouble appears to have persisted – and on both sides of the law. Eventually in October 1882, application was made for two particular special constables to be removed.

The line opened on March 10th 1884, and within a few years there was access to many additional routes. These included the SER Mid-Kent line when the Selsdon and Woodside line opened in August 1885, and to Tunbridge Wells via Edenbridge and Groombridge (opened October 1888). Although the Oxted line never really acquired 'main-line' status, it served for most of its life as a useful commuter and through passenger service.

A Tunbridge Wells-bound ex-SECR 'birdcage' set hauled by Class E5 SR No 2402 Radial Tank at Hurst Green Halt c1936. (Lens of Sutton)

Initial weekday services comprised four trains run by each company with the SER trains terminating at Oxted. By August, two of these used the loop at Crowhurst to reach Edenbridge and one to reach Tunbridge Junction (now Tonbridge). In 1885 the LBSCR ran four trains to East Grinstead plus three terminating at Oxted and another to Tunbridge Wells via East Grinstead on the Forest Row line. When the Groombridge line opened in 1888, LBSCR trains reached Tunbridge Wells by a shorter route using their own Edenbridge (now Edenbridge Town) station.

The first station on the Oxted line after leaving South Croydon was Selsdon. Opened as Selsdon Road in 1885, the station was built at the point where the new Woodside line joined the Oxted line in the same year. However, after spasmodic use through the years, Selsdon finally closed in June 1959. The Woodside–Selsdon link closed in May 1983.

Nearly a mile to the south, Sanderstead station has been served over the years by regular DEMU sets to East Grinstead and Uckfield as well as being a terminus for electric services from London Bridge using the newly electrified section from South Croydon to the site of Selsdon station. There were plans around 1927 for a narrow-gauge electric railway to be built from Sanderstead to Orpington, called the Southern Heights Light Railway, but the project never transpired.

In December 1986, British Rail announced that following bad damage by fire the previous June, Sanderstead station was scheduled for rebuilding at a cost of £250,000 with completion expected by summer, 1987. Sadly, the old signal box, an unusual feature in the centre of the down platform, was to be demolished.

Riddlesdown station, in a deep cutting leading to an 837 yard tunnel, opened in June 1927. This was as a result of local building development, supported of course by the newly-formed Southern Railway. Upper Warlingham opened with the line in 1884 but was known as 'Upper Warlingham and Whyteleafe' from 1894 to 1900. Once boasting numerous sidings, many were out of use by 1945 and others were gone by 1963.

Woldingham opened as 'Marden Park' but changed to its present name ten years after the line began. The nearby Marden Park acquired notoriety in the 1970s when the Government announced plans that the area might be considered as a terminus for the Channel Tunnel. Apparently the public outcry was such that the idea was abandoned.

Oxted has changed little since its opening although the platforms were lengthened at the up end in the 1960s. Like others on the line, most of its sidings have gone although a bay remains at the down end. For many years it has served as a place where the East Grinstead and Uckfield off-peak services combined or separated on their way to or from London Bridge.

After Hurst Green, opened as a wooden-built halt in 1907 and resited to become the present brick structure in 1961, comes the point where the East Grinstead and Uckfield lines separate.

Keeping on the East Grinstead route, Crowhurst Junction is soon reached, where a spur to the original SER line diverged to the left. Now completely removed, it once served trains to Tonbridge and beyond being particularly useful on the several occasions when Sevenoaks tunnel was under repair.

Lingfield seems to have been not only famous for its racecourse but also its bananas! After the Second World War, new traffic developed with the construction of a ripening shed for bananas off one of the sidings at the up end. A daily train of refrigerated vans, sometimes as many as twenty, became a frequent sight. Earlier in July 1898, authority had been given for a continuation of a siding to the racecourse itself but this was never built. However, a large extra footbridge was built at the down end leading to a covered way on the course. It was this footbridge which was recently removed and reinstated at Sheffield Park for use by Bluebell Railway enthusiasts.

In common with many rural stations, Lingfield was built some distance from its village. In the village centre can be found 'the cage', a small 'lock-up' last occupied in 1882 to hold a poacher overnight. But there was a time when the cell was a little more crowded. In 1850, no less than eleven poachers were held at the same time in cramped conditions although during the night there was a dramatic escape. While the police constable on duty dozed, the poachers' friends crept up in the dark and removed the roof to free the captives!

Dormans station, a mile or so to the south, has retained its elegant building, unusually built at right angles to the track. It has survived over a century with its round-headed windows and ornate chimneys. Gone, however, are the covered-ways to the platforms where only a shelter exists on the up side.

When electrification reached East Grinstead in October 1987, the line increased in importance. In addition plans are being considered at present by the privately owned Bluebell Railway to rebuild the track from Horsted Keynes to East Grinstead thus providing a station of their own adjacent to the BR platform. So, the Oxted line has a new lease of life. It is even possible that the stations along the route will see special Bluebell excursions directly through to Sheffield Park before too many years are out.

Chapter 15

EARLY DAYS AT GATWICK

Gatwick Racecourse station on the main London to Brighton line opened in 1891. A racecourse at the site had started earlier the same year and it was inevitable that the two should have close links.

Previous race meetings had been held in the Croydon area. There had been a racecourse at Stroud Green (see Chapter 11) but this had attracted so much traffic by road and rail that eventually an improved site 'in a quieter location' was chosen at Gatwick. In addition Croydon racecourse had become the scene of much rowdy behaviour from undesirable visitors and it closed in November 1890, whilst the new course was under construction.

The station at Gatwick Racecourse was completed in September 1891. To cater for the anticipated traffic, an up relief line was opened from Gatwick to Horley in October 1892. This line made it possible for Gatwick station to be considerably altered under the powers of an Act agreed in 1899 and, at the same time, a fourth line was added being an extension of the quadrupling to be carried out from Earlswood to Horley.

The racecourse owners had paid £5,000 to the railway authorities towards the construction of the station, which soon became an important part of the racecourse itself. The station

A down express passes through Gatwick Racecourse station in LBSCR days. The station became the present Gatwick Airport on May 27 1958. (Lens of Sutton)

initially served the course only, with frequent excursions on race-days. Three long covered walkways were constructed to the grandstand.

Not far from the grandstand stood a fine bandstand obviously a centre of much entertainment in the heyday of racing. This bandstand remains intact today but at its new site in the centre of Queens Square in the Crawley shopping precinct. It was purchased by the local council for a mere £60!

The racecourse achieved much fame throughout its life. During the First World War, the Grand National was transferred from Aintree to Gatwick for the years 1916 to 1918. By 1930, the valuable Grand National Trial was introduced, attracting many famous horses. Special Pullman excursion trains were run on race-days and Gatwick was a popular place indeed!

Around the same time new sounds were being heard overhead with aircraft, including an Avro 504 and a Gipsy Moth, taking to the air. The son of a builder in Redhill, called Waters, had started a flying club quite near the paddock. Flying, of course, expanded and soon the racing authorities were claiming that those wishing to enjoy a day at Gatwick could now arrive by road, rail or air.

This was not the first time the railways and the aerodrome had worked together. Since the First World War the railway lines had always proved a reliable – and often the only – navigational aid for aircraft. Pilots, often lost, would follow the Brighton line northwards as they looked for aerodromes to the south of London.

Soon farmland between the racecourse and nearby Lowfield Heath was bought to develop an aerodrome to be named Gatwick after the course itself. By September 1935, Tinsley Green rail-

Gatwick Airport station, August 1987. The platform signal box was removed as recently as 1982 to make way for escalators to the new overhead concourse. Today the Gatwick Express, seen waiting on the left, provides transport for around 5,000,000 passengers annually. (Author)

A general view of Gatwick Racecourse and grandstand in the early 1920s. In the foreground, the auctioneer's stand – the bandstand beyond is now in Queens Square, Crawley. (Pratt & Co., Haywards Heath)

way station opened near where the original beehive control tower still stands. The station was renamed Gatwick Airport on June 1st 1936. Racing continued until the early 1940s by which time the land had been taken over by the Government. With the country at war, priorities perhaps became confused when a final day of training on Spitfires had to be cancelled through a race meeting!

Before leaving the earlier Tinsley Green station it is worth recalling an account from J.H. Bentley's book, *Copthorne – People and Places*. Much has been heard in the recent past of 'The Great Train Robbers' but probably lesser known is the time when nearby Copthorne had its own 'train robbers' who were active in the area. The events go back to the 1930s when goods trains were frequently parked in a siding overnight. Not far away was the Radford Road railway bridge and it was here that certain 'adventurous groups' made frequent visits.

Stories have it that the practice was to lower a rope over the bridge parapet to where fellow conspirators were waiting below on the line and then goodies were hauled up such as bacon, sacks of sugar and similar items which had been stacked in the railway wagons. When completed, the 'robbers' would carry their loads entering Copthorne by a little used route. Apparently all went well for a considerable time until one night the police were waiting in a wood for the culprits. Arrests were made and the adventures of the 'Copthorne Train Robbers' came to an abrupt end.

Gatwick Racecourse station closed in 1935. The new Airport station opened on May 27th 1958, the day before the old airport station (near the Beehive) finally closed. The Beehive still survives of course and it has a 'ghost' as a reminder. A few years ago, workers in a hangar thought they saw a colleague walking towards them in a long, dark coat and trilby hat. But as he reached them he vanished, accompanied by a sudden and chilling drop in temperature. The old days are not forgotten . . .

From such modest beginnings at Gatwick, it is surely some achievement that today's trains from the airport can cater for around 30,000 passengers a day. British Rail's announcement in 1985 that the 'Gatwick Express', the link between London and Gatwick Airport, had broken all records in its first year surely came as no surprise. The fact that passenger numbers increased by 35% over the previous year compared with a growth of 12% in airport passengers, points out not only the increasing use of the airport but the growing popularity of the new service.

The Gatwick Express started services on May 14th 1984, running non-stop from Gatwick to London, scheduled to take 30 minutes for the journey with speeds of up to 90 mph. It is powered by a Class 73 electro-diesel push-pull locomotive and the coaches are inter-city Mark II stock with modifications for the push-pull arrangement. The train is distinctive with its livery of dark and light grey, red and white and the coaches are fitted with automatic interior sliding doors. It is estimated that the express provides transport for some 5 million passengers annually and from its launch to June 1987 over 14 million people have used the service.

Following a local government re-organisation in 1974, Gatwick left Surrey to become part of Sussex. But this would hardly be justification for not including the station and airport in a Surrey book.

Today there are only a few reminders of the early times. It is still possible to make out part of the first airport station 500 yards south of the present station. And the old concrete passenger bridge that once spanned this station now crosses the track at Balcombe station in Sussex, 7 miles to the south.

Gatwick Airport station in its more casual days! This is the first airport station opened as Tinsley Green in 1935. (Lens of Sutton)

Chapter 16

TRAINS REACH TATTENHAM CORNER

A journey on the Tattenham Corner branch today shows only too sadly how decline has long since set in. Along the line many station buildings are shuttered, waiting rooms have closed and canopies have been removed. Tattenham Corner's once proud six platforms were reduced to three as early as November 1970, at a time when most of the sidings had already disappeared. Staff only seem to be available at peak periods – all this a far cry from the days when each station had its own station-master plus porters and signalmen.

First moves for a branch up the Chipstead Valley came in the late 1860s. The LCDR had a plan to build a railway south from East Croydon, using running powers over LBSCR lines as far as Stoats Nest (later Coulsdon North) and then curving up the valley towards Tadworth. From there the line would curve towards Banstead where tracks would fork left and right to either Epsom Downs or Sutton. No doubt through lack of finance and also lack of enthusiasm from the LBSCR, who claimed it to be their 'territory', the idea foundered.

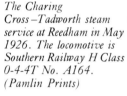

The Charing Cross–Tadworth steam service at Reedham in May 1926. The locomotive is Southern Railway H Class 0-4-4T No. A164. (Pamlin Prints)

In the book *The Tattenham Corner Branch*, N. Owen writes that the branch probably owes its existence initially to pressure from farmers in the 1880s who were becoming increasingly dissatisfied with the difficulties of cartage to farms throughout the area. Goods facilities were available at Banstead on the LBSCR Epsom Downs line but it was a fair distance from Banstead's yard to reach such places as Tadworth or Kingswood.

The idea received support from wealthy residents in the

Kingswood Warren area. The scheme was master-minded by an MP called Cosmo Bonsor, a Director of the Bank of England. It was soon appreciated that a railway serving the district would increase the value of the land and prices would inflate very much to the landowners' advantage. Bonsor and his friends first proposed a spur from the Epsom Downs branch at Drift Bridge to reach a point near the present Tadworth station. It would be known as the Epsom Downs Extension Railway for which capital of £65,000 was required, the majority having been already offered by Bonsor himself.

Opposition came from a local landowner who claimed his land would be cut in two. The Epsom Grandstand Association also complained. They said that the line would cross a new 'straight mile' they were proposing and horses would be adversely affected. However, the idea was never taken up but it did pave the way for the more practical scheme which was to follow.

The Chipstead Valley Railway was estimated at £250,000 for a line from Purley to Tattenham Corner. The company was formed to build the branch as far as Tadworth and the Epsom Downs Extension Company would cover the track to the terminus.

Eventually a single line from Purley to 'Kingswood and Burgh Heath' opened on November 2nd 1897, although records indicate that trains actually started a week later. The only intermediate station was 'Chipstead and Banstead Downs'. Purley had been rebuilt as a six-platform station partly because quadrupling towards Redhill was in hand (see Chapter 17) and also to accommodate separately the branch line trains.

In January 1899, the SER and LCDR amalgamated to become known as the SECR. Bonsor became the Chairman of the SECR Managing Committee and continued also to control the SER.

In the same year rivalry between the SECR and the LBSCR was further aggravated when the SECR considered building a link from the Oxted line near Sanderstead (jointly SECR/

LBSCR owned) through a 580 yard tunnel under the Downs to join the Caterham and Tattenham Corner lines south of Purley at a new SECR Purley station! History shows of course that the idea failed.

By July 1st 1900, trains were reaching 'Tadworth and Walton-on-the-Hill' and four months later the branch was doubled. Between Tadworth and 'Kingswood and Burgh Heath' were two short tunnels, built because of local objections to open cuttings through common land. One tunnel was called 'Kingswood' and the other acquired the delightful name of 'Hoppity'!

It was of course appropriate that Tattenham Corner station should open on Derby Day – June 4th 1901! On that occasion it was recorded that the terminus handled between 14,000 and 15,000 passengers. Many came from the London stations but large numbers arrived in special excursions from the coast or through Reading. The passengers were delighted. Here was a new railway service which took its punters right to the racecourse

itself. In addition to this a raised lawn close to the station gave excellent views over much of the Downs.

Tattenham Corner station in busier times! Steam Pullman specials wait for returning race day crowds c1922. (Lens of Sutton)

Three years after the line's opening, a station opened at Smitham close to Coulsdon North station (then Stoats Nest) on the Brighton line. Despite apparent duplication of services, the site was important historically since not far away the line crossed the route of the Surry Iron Railway, which had opened just under one hundred years previously (Chapter 1).

On race-days, services to Tattenham Corner were in great demand but efforts to encourage ordinary passenger traffic to the terminus were less successful. Because of this the station closed for ordinary services from September 1914 and trains terminated at Tadworth. Otherwise the line remained busy and in 1911 Reedham Halt opened, close to Old Lodge Lane, Purley. The halt took its name from the orphanage at the top of the nearby hill.

Army camps were set up on Epsom Downs during the First World War and the branch saw only military trains. Tattenham Corner was used for munitions work and after the war the station had a strange role when surplus ROD engines returning from France were auctioned off there.

The 1920s proved an important era for the branch. On Derby Day 1923, around 40,000 people passed through Tattenham Corner station. Among the additional trains running there were many all-Pullman specials. In addition in the 1920s, the Royal Train switched from Epsom Downs to Tattenham Corner to become a regular attender on Derby Days.

Third rail electric trains came to the Caterham/Tattenham Corner branches on the March 25th 1928. Tattenham Corner station was re-opened to normal services and the platforms at Reedham Halt, Chipstead and Kingswood were lengthened to take the new 9-car trains. Woodmansterne station opened in July 1932 and four years later Reedham Halt was upgraded to become

WD 2-8-0 locomotives back from the First World War front await sale at Tattenham Corner in 1919. (Lens of Sutton)

known as Reedham.

There is no record of any major dislocation of services during the Second World War. However, shortly afterwards on October 24th 1947, there was a serious accident when a Tattenham Corner/Caterham train carrying about 1,000 passengers crashed in thick fog into the back of a Haywards Heath train near South Croydon station. The mishap, caused by signalman's error, cost thirty two lives and many injured.

Despite the improved prosperity following electrification, a decline set in, probably from the late 1950s when services were generally reduced. Most of the sidings had gone by the early 1960s and most off-peak trains were reduced to two cars. Many trains worked as shuttle services to and from Purley. Soon booking offices were opened at peak times only with fares collected aboard trains at other times. There was a respite in decline when, following passengers' protests, some through services were restored from May 1970, to Croydon and London. Even so, there must be many today who wonder what the future of the branch holds in store.

Finally a recollection from the halcyon days of the early 1920s. It was not surprising that with Cosmo Bonsor resident at Kingswood Warren, Kingswood and Burgh Heath station should be a most elegant affair. The station house was three-storey and above the platform was a canopy also used as an open-air tea terrace. Unfortunately the novelty quickly wore off since tea and cakes to the accompaniment of soot and steam were obviously not to everybody's taste!

Chapter 17

THE BRIGHTON LINE – QUADRUPLING AND THE QUARRY LINE

When the SER opened lines eastwards in 1842 and westwards in 1849 from the station now known as Redhill, traffic on the line from Croydon southwards increased considerably. Chapter 2 related how this section had been built by the L&BR but an Act of Parliament dated 1839 had stipulated that part of the stretch should be sold to the SER. Bitter rows had followed and usage of the line by the Brighton company required special payments to the rival company. With both companies now using the line, relations grew worse and there was even talk of the SER blocking Brighton trains by giving preference to their own.

In February 1869 an Agreement was signed whereby the payments to the SER would be based on the Brighton company's gross receipts and a figure of £14,000 a year was accepted. It was a 10 year agreement and when renewal was considered in 1879, there was further trouble. The SER complained that it could not improve its services covering the new routes because there were too many Brighton trains. In addition the LBSCR was unhappy because its trains were not allowed to stop at Merstham, the only intermediate SER station between Coulsdon and Redhill.

The Quarry line which opened to passenger traffic in April 1900 seen near Hooley in February 1987. To the right the original London–Brighton line of 1841. (Author)

Finally, after continued arguments between the companies, Henry (later Sir Henry) Oakley, General Manager of the Great Northern Railway, was asked to arbitrate. This he did in July 1889 with the result that the LBSCR's payments to the SER were increased to £20,000 a year.

Meanwhile in 1888, quadrupling (widening to four tracks) from South Croydon to Coulsdon (later Coulsdon South) had been considered by the LBSCR directors in order to provide independent tracks for their trains. In 1890 the company received a resolution from the Brighton Council urging the widening of the line as far as Redhill to overcome the traffic problems. Two years later an estimate to double the line from Croydon to Redhill was put at £370,000. Plans were prepared and a Bill was deposited in November 1893. There was of course very little opposition from the SER which could only benefit from the project and its only complaint was that the new LBSCR line might interfere with the SER station at Coulsdon. In addition, the LBSCR agreed to meet the London County Council request that its stretch of line through Cane Hill Asylum should be a covered-way.

Parliament gave the go-ahead for the widening of lines from South Croydon to Redhill in July 1894. The Coulsdon-Redhill section was to be 6 miles 48 chains in length being described as a new 'avoiding' line (later to be called the Quarry line). Engineering works were very heavy. Most of the track, much of it parallel to the original SER line, was either in a cutting, on an embankment or in a tunnel. South from Coulsdon, two bridges were needed to cross and recross the main Brighton Road (A23) and between the bridges the line crossed the Cane Hill Asylum (now

Stoats Nest station (which later became Coulsdon North) not long after its opening on this site in November 1899. (Lens of Sutton)

Cane Hill Hospital) grounds. The track was located in a cutting which, the Act stipulated, should be temporarily fenced before and during construction. Brick side walls were built which were roofed over and the ground replaced on top. It was not until 1954 that the 'Cane Hill Covered Way' (as it became known) was opened out to save maintenance costs. By this time there were no objections since engine smoke was no longer a problem.

In 1896 there was an unexpected move from the SER which suggested a new line from Merstham to Brighton to compete with what it considered to be the 'unsatisfactory LBSCR services'. The route proposed was to be to the west of the Brighton main line passing through Charlwood, Colgate and Plummers Plain, near Horsham. Southwards it would pass between Bolney and Cowfold in Sussex to reach Brighton via Newtimber. An advan-

A train on the Quarry line passes the remains of Coulsdon North station which closed in October 1983. (Author)

tage claimed was that no tunnelling was thought to be needed. The scheme of course came to nothing and in any event it was contrary to the SER/LBSCR 1848 Agreement over territories.

On November 5th 1899, two new stations were opened being Purley Oaks, between South Croydon and Purley, and Stoats Nest (later Coulsdon North). Stoats Nest, a terminus for local trains also incorporating numerous carriage sidings, was conveniently sited just before tracks left to join the new 'avoiding' line. During work on the 'avoiding' line, massive quantities of chalk became available and much of this was needed for embankments south of the new Merstham tunnel. Chalk was also used to provide the additional embankments between Croydon and

Coulsdon with further amounts being disposed of by filling used gravel pits locally.

Finally the new line from Coulsdon to Earlswood (by-passing Redhill) was ready for use. South of Coulsdon it was officially called the Through Line because with no intermediate stations it was planned only fast trains would be used. It was not long, however, before it became known as the Quarry line since at the south end of the new Merstham tunnel, the line ran immediately adjacent to the quarry that had been the southern end of the CM&G Iron Railway. Although freight traffic began on November 5th 1899, passenger trains could not start until April 1st 1900 by which time three intermediate signal boxes had been completed.

J.T. Howard Turner wrote in his book, '*The LBSCR – Completion and Maturity*' that he had heard on more than one occasion of a connecting passage built between the two Merstham tunnels. Had it existed, the passage would have been a steep one for the new tunnel was built about 25 feet higher than the original one and surely the purpose of such a link would need to be questioned anyway. With the tunnels under separate company ownership, the possibility seems remote, nevertheless such stories appear to have persisted.

With the Quarry line open the LBSCR and SER overcrowding troubles seemed to be resolved. Naturally consideration had already been given to quadrupling track further southwards and to this end authority had been given in August 1899 for widening works between Earlswood and the north end of Balcombe tunnel. By April 1902, there were plans to extend from Balcombe to Burgess Hill in Sussex and an estimate was received covering the

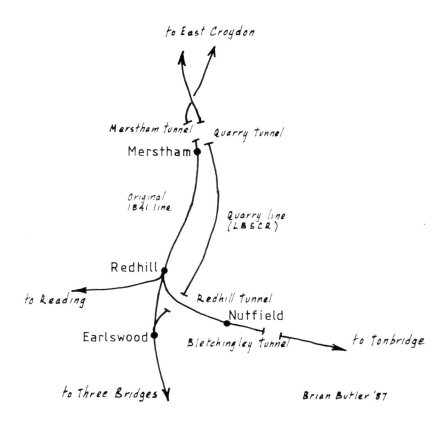

to East Croydon

Merstham tunnel   Quarry tunnel

Merstham

Original
1841 line

Quarry line
(LBSCR)

Redhill

to Reading

Redhill tunnel
Nutfield

Earlswood   Bletchingley tunnel   to Tonbridge

to Three Bridges   Brian Butler '87

Hassocks to Preston Park section. The schemes were ambitious with ideas to rebuild Haywards Heath station plus a £70,000 fly-over junction at Keymer Junction (south of Wivelsfield station). A Bill was deposited and authority to go ahead between Balcombe tunnel and Keymer Junction was received in July 1903. No doubt concerned at the cost and the prospect of building duplicate tunnels at Balcombe and Haywards Heath, and also the task of widening the Ouse Viaduct (proposed on the west side), the railway company soon forgot its pipe-dream. Three years later in 1906, a further Bill was approved to quadruple between Balcombe and the north end of the Ouse Viaduct, but even this came to nothing.

During these considerations, work had been proceeding on the widening from Earlswood to Balcombe tunnel. Earlswood and Three Bridges stations were extended as required and Horley station was completely rebuilt on a new site to the south of the existing one. The Earlswood to Three Bridges widening came into use in 1907 and the stretch to Balcombe Tunnel Junction was opened on May 22nd 1910.

Chapter 18

BRANCHES TO HAMPTON COURT, SHEPPERTON AND CHESSINGTON

When Cardinal Wolsey began building Hampton Court Palace on the banks of the Thames in the early 16th century, he little realised that about 450 years later some half million people annually would be arriving at a nearby railway station to view it. When the line first opened on February 1st 1849, horse traction was used – quite a contrast to today's half-hourly electric service from Waterloo.

The branch to Hampton Court left the main line to Woking west of Surbiton and was less then two miles long. It had little support from W.J. Chaplin, the LSWR Chairman, when initially considered but the line went ahead because it was thought 'a public necessity – affording a fresh means of cheap and legitimate recreation to the poorer classes'. His doubts were soon dispelled, however, for by 1865, 13 of the 47 main line departures from Waterloo were for Hampton Court.

An Act to build the line had been passed on July 16th 1846.

An early picture of Hampton Court station building in LSWR days. (Lens of Sutton)

Engineer Joseph Locke immediately recommended extending to Windsor joining the line from Weybridge at Staines. A further branch from the Weybridge line at Chertsey to Ascot racecourse was also considered. Meantime the Windsor, Staines & South

Western Company had applied for a line from Staines via Egham to the LSWR main line at Pirbright Junction and, although this was never built, construction of the Hampton Court branch had been delayed. Finally, despite financial restrictions because of the post-Railway Mania depression, work started in January 1848.

There was one intermediate station at Thames Ditton which opened in 1851/2 (no precise date recorded). Much of the line was built on a continuous embankment but levelled off near the Thames at Hampton Court Bridge. The station, at one time advertised 'For East and West Molesey', was built of deep red brick in semi-Jacobean style with decorated windows, corners and doors plus extravagant gable ends. When services began, five trains ran each way daily taking about 45 minutes to or from Waterloo.

In July 1915, the Hampton Court flying junction was opened carrying the branch down-line over four main lines. Despite the problems of the First World War, the construction was a considerable achievement with the main girders each 160 feet long and each weighing 85 tons. Third-rail electrification came one year

LSWR Class M7 No. 378 (built 1903) with passenger set at Hampton Court station c1910. (Lens of Sutton)

later in June 1916, when the line from Malden to Hampton Court was completed.

The six and a half mile branch line to Shepperton from the New Malden–Twickenham line had the distinction of being one of the first to use the new LSWR third-rail electric trains. At a time when the LBSCR was going ahead with its 'overhead electrics' (Chapter 4), LSWR engineer Herbert Jones had visited America with the result that the direct current third-rail system was used.

After running such a service between Waterloo and East Putney from October 25th 1915, electric trains reached Shepperton on January 30th 1916. Coaches were the usual compartment

Shepperton station, which opened on November 1 1864, seen in Southern Railway days. (Lens of Sutton)

type with steam coaches having been converted for electric traction. They were made up into three coach sets with each end-coach having one motor bogie.

When the Shepperton line first opened on November 1st 1864, there had been many previous contenders to reach the area. In 1861 a company called the Metropolitan & Thames Valley Railway (M&TVR) had agreed that a line should be built to connect Isleworth, Richmond, Twickenham and Shepperton via the LSWR and the GWR. A prospectus issued said that London workers 'from the overcrowded and unhealthy portion of the City . . .' should more easily reach healthier localities. Furthermore it was considered that the line to Shepperton should continue to north of Chertsey Bridge to 'capture' traffic from Weybridge but this idea was soon dropped.

Inter-company squabbles ensued with the M&TVR breaking with the GWR over financial matters and turning to the LSWR who in the past had been anxious to keep broad-gauge trains out of the area at any cost. The Shepperton branch was finally authorised by an Act of July 17th 1862, with the M&TVR now restyled the Thames Valley Railway (TVR). Exactly one year later, agreement was finalised allowing the LSWR to work the proposed single track line to Shepperton indefinitely in return for expenses and payments to the TVR. In a further development, the TVR and LSWR prepared a joint bill to extend the branch to Weybridge but the latter decided against this considering it to be a scheme to poach their main line traffic and the idea was dropped.

When services to Shepperton began, there were seven passenger trains each way daily and four on Sundays. There was soon agitation to provide a faster service to London and although there was some improvement and more trains provided, the journey still took almost an hour. On July 5th 1865, an Act was

passed authorising the LSWR to acquire the company. Attempts still continued locally for the line to be extended to link with the Chertsey branch but without success. A later LSWR plan of 1885 also failed.

Intermediate stations were Fulwell, Hampton and Sunbury. The line was doubled as far as Fulwell around 1867, but efforts in 1877 to establish a station at Kempton Park near an intended racecourse were refused by the LSWR to avoid further doubling. Eventually in September 1878, the LSWR gave way and a private member's platform was provided on the down side. A year later an up platform was approved with the racecourse company paying half the cost. Meanwhile doubling of the track continued with Shepperton reached by December 9th 1878. At Sunbury there were problems when passengers complained in 1886 of (among other things) a nuisance caused by manure traffic! In 1894 a curve was completed which allowed direct running from Shepperton towards Kingston.

It is fitting that on a siding near Shepperton station there is a Pullman car which is today used by the railway book publishers, Ian Allan Ltd. The coach *Malaga* was purchased from the Pullman Car Company in 1963 and was located on a small section of track round which the company's Head Office building 'Terminal House' was subsequently constructed. In 1949 the coach was completely refurbished for use by King George VI for journeys on BR Southern Region. It was also used on the Golden Arrow service between Victoria and Dover.

Whilst in the area the old village of Shepperton is worth a visit. The central square has two old inns, the *Anchor*, with a carved oak porch, and the *King's Head* with a modern sign showing the head of Charles II. This keeps alive the legend that he stayed there with Nell Gwynne.

Chessington branch on the Raynes Park to Epsom line opened on May 28th 1939, being one of the few to be opened with electric track. Originally the Southern Railway had intended it should be a loop leaving the Raynes Park line at Motspur Park and rejoining the same line north of Leatherhead. Parliamentary approval had been given in 1930 but by the time Chessington South had been reached, the threat of war stopped any further progress southwards and in 1961 the Green Belt scheme stopped any building development south of the now established terminus.

Work on the branch started in 1936 and within two years Tolworth was reached with an intermediate station at Malden Manor. Construction had included a 140 ft viaduct over the Hogsmill River. The remainder of the branch was completed exactly one year later. Much of the line was built on an embankment and all four stations were constructed mainly of concrete in what was then no doubt considered a futuristic style.

The line has proved a busy one particularly for travellers to the well-known Chessington Zoo which covers a 65 acre site south of the terminus. Here children (and grown-ups?) can delight at the spectacle of over one thousand individual animals. Features include a Great Ape House, a Reptile House, a Pets' Corner and, of course, a miniature railway. It is perhaps less known that the zoo occupies the site of Burnt Stub, a 14th century house burned down to a 'stub' by Parliamentarians during the Civil War.

The Chessington branch suffered a serious accident in thick fog at the Motspur Park end of the line on November 6th 1947. Due to a signalling error, a train from Holmwood ran into the side of a busy evening Waterloo–Chessington South commuter train as it crossed on to the branch. Four passengers were killed and a number injured.

Chessington branch line was the last to be constructed by Sir Herbert Walker's Southern Railway and remains today a fine example of a futuristic railway of the late 1930s.

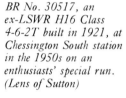

BR No. 30517, an ex-LSWR H16 Class 4-6-2T built in 1921, at Chessington South station in the 1950s on an enthusiasts' special run. (Lens of Sutton)

CONCLUSION

The decline of many Surrey lines commenced during the 1920s. Buses were on the increase providing a more flexible service than the trains. In addition, road haulage was on the increase. Yet unlike its neighbouring counties, Surrey has to date suffered few actual line closures.

The county's main loss was in June 1965 when the branch from Horsham to Guildford closed. With bus services available throughout the area, the line no longer served a useful purpose. Similarly as recently as 1983, the short branch from Woodside to Selsdon closed. With passenger traffic having continually decreased over the years, the line could hardly be justified.

A major factor contributing to the decline of the railways was the elimination of competition between private companies brought about by 'grouping' in 1923. This had the effect of merging more than 100 existing companies throughout Great Britain into four main companies: LNER (London & North Eastern Railway); LMS (London Midland & Scottish Railway); GWR (Great Western Railway); and SR (Southern Railway).

Meantime changes were taking place which were to materially affect the railways and their future. With living standards rising and paid holidays becoming an accepted condition of work, people were willing to live further from their place of work. Electricity was becoming more freely available and, with the coalfields of the North no longer vital to industry, people were migrating southwards. The Home Counties became a popular area bringing with it the need to provide extensive surburban rail services between the capital and the surrounding districts.

It was in this climate that the Southern Railway developed its electric services. An AC overhead system had already been inherited from its predecessors, the LBSCR, providing services as far south as Coulsdon North and Sutton. In 1926, the present DC system was adopted and by 1928, 'third rail' electrics were installed along the old SER lines to Caterham and Tattenham Corner. Eventually, threatened by effective coach and motorcar competition between London and Brighton, electric trains were provided to the coast. During the next few years, electrification extended rapidly throughout much of the network to be halted only when The Second World War began. Planned work on the Oxted line to East Grinstead was shelved.

The war effectively wrecked the finances of the railways which were to be saved by nationalisation in 1948. With Government subsidies involved it was inevitable that 'rationalisation' processes would follow. Managemment of the main-line railways was delegated by the British Transport Commission to the Railway Executive with the Southern Region taking charge of all lines in the South. But progress to commence capital investment programmes was slow due to material shortages. In addition integration with other forms of transport, a declared aim of nationalisation, made little headway.

In 1953 there were changes. A Transport Act aimed at decentralization dissolved the Railway Executive and from January 1955 the Southern Region was controlled by a Board, responsible to the Commission, but with considerable freedom to determine its own actions. Three Divisions were created, the 'South Eastern', 'South Western', and 'Central'. Whereas the SER and the LSWR had to some extent regained their old titles, the Board regretted that neither 'Brighton' nor 'South Coast' after the LBSCR could be included.

Despite optimistic plans for redevelopment, freight traffic was on the decline and the railways were becoming more dependent on passenger traffic. By the early 1960s, the Government's attitude had hardened. In a further Transport Act of 1962, it was clear that commercial viability was considered a more important factor than providing a service to the public. In 1963 the Transport Commission was dissolved and a new Railways Board created. At the same time, the Minister of Transport appointed the Stedeford Group to look at the future of the railways. The findings were not published but one of its members was Dr Richard Beeching (later Lord Beeching), a name that was to become very well known in the years to come.

In March 1963 proposals were made in a report which became popularly known as the 'Beeching Plan'. Basically the idea was to keep lines considered suitable to rail traffic and give up the remainder. It had been calculated that one third of the rail system in Britain carried only 1% of the total traffic! The report was considered disappointing in ignoring the potential of many Southern lines, particularly related to electrification. Also by planning the closure of many freight depots, it was thought the report failed to foresee the future of container traffic in the region. Line singling, 'bus-stop' type stations for economy and the use of diesel-electric locomotives were other aspects considered overlooked at the time.

At the present time continuing financial losses on the railways appear inevitable. Perhaps there is comfort in the fact that further widespread closures on the scale previously suffered would be politically unacceptable today. Presumably Government subsidies will continue and, will no doubt, increase in the years to come.

In February 1987 BR announced plans to produce duel system trains, able to use either the overhead wires of the Midland Region or the third-rail electrification of the Southern. Is it possible that 'overhead electrics' might be seen in Surrey again similar in principle to those which reached Coulsdon North and Sutton in April 1925 then lasting only four and a half years?

INDEX

BIBLIOGRAPHY

In compiling *Surrey Railways Remembered*, I have referred to numerous sources which include the following and which can be recommended for further reading:

Vic Mitchell & Keith Smith	Southern Main Lines – Epsom to Horsham	Middleton Press
Geoffrey Body	Railways of the Southern Region	Patrick Stephens Ltd
H.P. White	A Regional History of the Railways of Great Britain Vol. 2 Southern England	David and Charles
H.P. White	Forgotten Railways: South East England	David and Charles
W.B. Herbert	Railways Ghosts	David and Charles
R.A. Williams A.M. Inst.T.	The London and South Western Railway Vol. 1 The Formative Years Vol. 2 Growth and Consolidation	David and Charles
C.F. Dendy Marshall Revised by R.W. Kidner	History of the Southern Railway	Ian Allan Ltd.
J.T. Howard Turner	The London, Brighton and South Coast Railway Vol. 1 Origins and Formation Vol. 2 Establishment and Growth Vol. 3 Completion and Maturity	B.T. Batsford Ltd.

Dr Edwin Course	The Railways of Southern England: The Main Lines The Secondary and Branch Lines Independent and Light Railways	B.T. Batsford Ltd.
Derek Bayliss	Retracing the First Public Railway	Living History Publications, Croydon
Brian J. Salter	Epsom Town, Downs and Common	Living History Publications, Croydon
Peter A. Harding & John M. Clarke	The Bisley Camp Branch Line	Peter A. Harding, Woking
Jeoffry Spence	Caterham through the Centuries, from 'Caterham and Warlingham – Jubilee History'	The Bourne Society
Jeoffry Spence	The Caterham Railway	Oakwood Press
N. Owen	The Tattenham Corner Branch	Oakwood Press
R.W. Kidner	The Reading to Tonbridge line	Oakwood Press
Adrian Gray	The London to Brighton line	Oakwood Press
J.R.W. Kirkby	The Banstead & Epsom Downs Railway	Oakwood Press
H.R. Hodd	The Horsham – Guildford Direct Railway	Oakwood Press
C. Hamilton Ellis	The London Brighton & South Coast Railway	Ian Allan Ltd.
John King and Geoffrey Tait	Golden Gatwick	Royal Aeronautical Society, Gatwick Branch, and the BAA